WHEN THE SKY BREAKS

HURRICANES, TORNADOES, AND THE WORST WEATHER IN THE WORLD

SIMON
WHEN THE

WINCHESTER
SKY BREAKS

HURRICANES, TORNADOES, AND THE WORST WEATHER IN THE WORLD

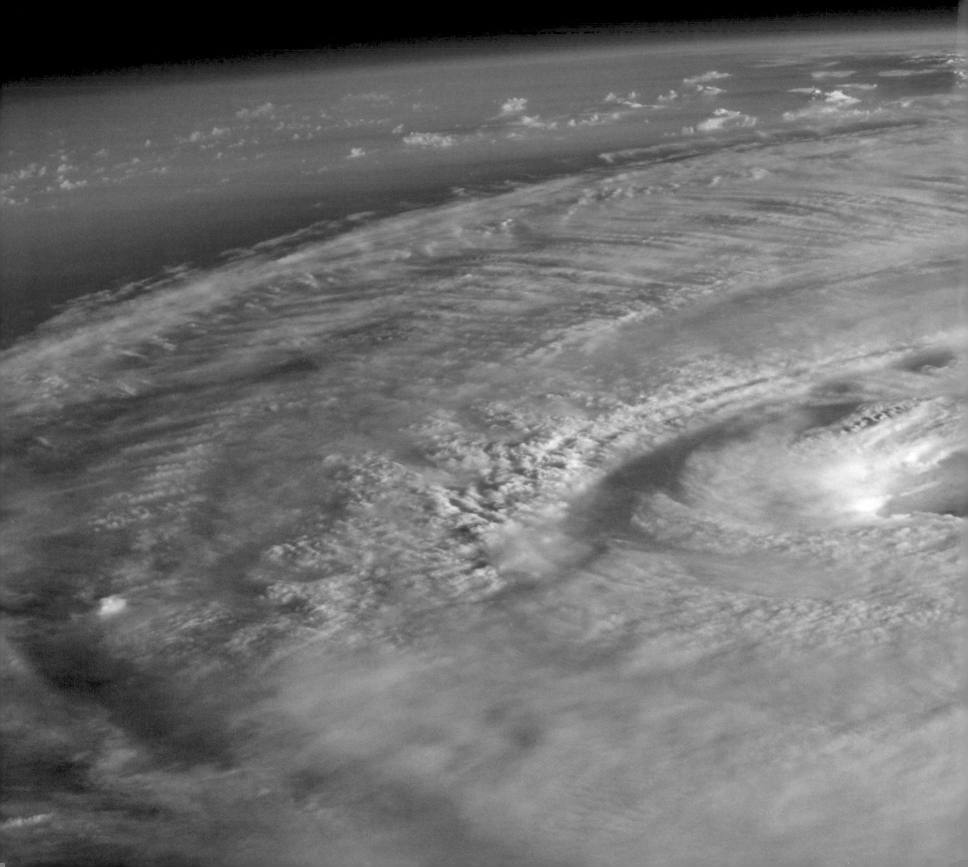

For Harriet.

Placetne, Magistra?

VIKING
An imprint of Penguin Random House LLC
375 Hudson Street
New York, New York 10014

First published in the United States
of America by Viking, an imprint of
Penguin Random House LLC, 2017

Smithsonian
This trademark is owned by the Smithsonian Institution and is
registered in the U.S. Patent and Trademark Office.

Smithsonian Enterprises:
Christopher Liedel, President
Carol LeBlanc, Senior Vice President, Education and Consumer Products
Brigid Ferraro, Vice President, Education and Consumer Products
Ellen Nanney, Licensing Manager
Kealy Gordon, Product Development Manager

Smithsonian National Museum of Natural History:
Dr. Don E. Wilson, Curator Emeritus, Department of Vertebrate Zoology

Copyright © 2017 by Simon Winchester,
Penguin Random House LLC, and Smithsonian Institution

LIBRARY OF CONGRESS CATALOGING-IN-PUBLICATION DATA IS AVAILABLE
ISBN 9780451476357

Manufactured in China   Designed by Jim Hoover
Set in Baskerville MT Std and Mynaruse Royale

10   9   8   7   6   5   4   3   2   1

CONTENTS

INTRODUCTION

Weather Lessons from an Ill Wind

The man calling said he knew I was interested in weather.

He was quite right. I had been for a long while. I had lived in India and written about the fascinating phenomenon of the summer rains called the monsoon. I had ventured to one of the world's hottest places, a town called Jacobabad in Pakistan, where I fried an egg on the hood of my car; and then the wettest, a village in eastern India called Mawsynram, where people wear knups, large woven bamboo-and-leaf umbrellas that cover their heads and much of their bodies. I had also sailed in a small boat around South Africa and written about the freak winds and waves you encounter south of Madagascar. And I was supposed to know a thing or two about whirlpools, since I had once gone around the world

reporting on the best and fiercest of them. So yes, I agreed with the magazine editor calling. I was indeed interested in weather—and I became *very interested* in the assignment he then proposed: I should follow the birth, growth, and effect of a big Atlantic Ocean hurricane and then write ten thousand words about it.

"Go to the very place," he said, "where a hurricane first forms—as a little ripple of winds in West Africa, a dust devil in the Sahara Desert. Watch as it then develops over the Cape Verde islands of the eastern Atlantic. Stick with it as it becomes a proper tropical storm, a circulating body of wind somewhere over the middle of the ocean. Keep going with the storm as it turns into something more dangerous, a small actual hurricane in the eastern Caribbean—which

Storm clouds over Grande Riviere, Trinidad, which developed into Hurricane Isaac (August 2012).

1

A ship's barometer is a three-foot-long (one-meter-long) contraption made of wood and glass and tubes, and mounted in gimbals (pivoted supports) so it doesn't roll with the movement of a ship.

could mature into a fully fledged high-category storm in the western Caribbean" (by which time, with luck, I'd be home safe and sound).

I started reading, researching, and planning, the timing being crucial. (I remembered the old mariners' mantra from my sailing days about when the big late-summer storms blow in the Caribbean Sea: *June—too soon. July—stand by. August—if you must. September—remember. October—all over.*) I would set off for Africa in May, then work my way back westward across the ocean through June, and I'd be in position in the Caribbean in July when storm season would be in full swing.

And then, like storms are wont to do, the assignment fizzled out. The editor decided it was too expensive. He told me on the day I was supposed to leave for Africa. I was devastated. This would have been an amazing article to research, and a great challenge to write.

But this cloud (since we are talking about atmospheric phenomena) had a decidedly silver lining. All the reading I had done for the ill-fated hurricane story transformed a topic I was mildly interested in to one I was now fully captivated by: the subject of weather. (One of the many benefits of working as a writer, a calling that involves learning something new every day.)

Over the years since, I have festooned my little house and garden in western Massachusetts with the tools of the trade

In a westerly wind, the cow's face on my weather vane points to the west. I have long thought it a curious convention that a wind's direction is always the direction it is coming from, while an ocean current's direction is where it is going to. So the cold current that brings all the fogs to San Francisco is said to be a southerly current, since it is heading from north to south, while a bitter wind that brings Arctic gales down from Newfoundland to New York City is said to be a nor'easter, since it is coming from the northeast. The fact that it is heading to the southwest isn't relevant, not to a meteorologist, at least.

of a very amateur meteorologist. There was already an ancient cow-shaped weather vane on top of the big barn, with the beast's nose pointing in the wind's direction: that was a start.

The first piece of real meteorological equipment I would own came as a birthday present from my parents. It was a quite splendid barograph, a lovely old-fashioned-looking confection of brass and teak and glass made by a firm in England. A barograph is a tool for measuring atmospheric pressure and recording it on paper. It has a clockwork-powered and slowly rotating brass drum, protected and visible inside a glass-walled box, and a complicated-looking arrangement of levers and vacuum tubes, and a rod with a pen at its end that records changes on the slow-moving paper wrapped around the revolving drum. The device marks steady changes in

atmospheric pressure as it rises and falls through the hours of the day and the days of the week during each seven-day period.

So my first job early each Sunday morning is to change my barograph paper. I carefully lift the glass case off the instrument, gently move the pen away from the recording paper, and detach the drum and unclasp the roll of paper with its long blue wavering ink line of the week's recorded pressure. On this I then write brief notes beside the trace, telling the atmospheric history of the seven days just past. So if on the previous Tuesday, say, the line of pressure had dipped sharply, then I would look in my weather diary and see that on Tuesday there had been a powerful thunderstorm, and I would be able to line up the two events. Then, beside the steep fall I would see on the barograph paper, I would

A barograph like this records, on a paper chart wrapped around the brass cylinder at left, the rise and fall of atmospheric pressure. I change the paper once a week.

write *high winds and rain* and put the paper away in a file. You begin to understand weather quite well when you keep an eye on atmospheric pressure—for pressure, as we will see later on, is the key to most things weather-related.

As my weather obsession took further hold, I bought a ship's barometer. Unlike a baro*graph*, which writes a record of atmospheric pressure on a piece of paper, a baro*meter* measures this pressure without writing it; and it does so very simply, by employing a vacuum tube that holds up a column of liquid mercury.

A barometer works like this: If you insert a thin vacuum tube into an open bowl of mercury, the liquid will move up the tube. It will in effect be sucked up the tube, but only to a certain height—up to about 30 inches, or 760 millimeters, in normal conditions. This is because the atmosphere has pressure that is pushing down on the surface of the mercury

in the bowl and forcing it up into the vacuum tube. This atmospheric pressure varies from day to day, and indeed from hour to hour. If rain is coming, for example, the pressure often drops—sometimes quite suddenly. When the pressure drops, the level of mercury in the tube will go down. If you have a barometer, you can see this drop (or rise) and can make rough forecasts as to what the weather outside is going to do.

When you buy an old-fashioned device like a ship's barometer, it comes without any mercury in it, for safety reasons. Mercury, a heavy liquid metal, is very poisonous; plus if it leaked in transit, the cleanup bills would be enormous. So when I bought my barometer, I also had to order five pounds of liquid mercury. This was quite tricky, requiring permits, specially made containers, and even house inspections. In the end I did get a tiny bottle of mercury . . . which seemed to weigh a ton. I very carefully filled the reservoir at the base of my barometer, inserted the long glass vacuum tube, and then watched, with great satisfaction, as the bright column of shining silver liquid climbed up and up and up until it settled at exactly 760 millimeters. I then gingerly lifted the device and suspended it from a hook on the wall—where it now faithfully notes the rises and falls in the pressure outside. Mercury is slightly sticky and can adhere to the barometer's glass tube, so I tap it each time I leave home, just to give me a rough idea of whether it would be prudent to take my umbrella. If the mercury level drops, then the atmospheric pressure is dropping, and rain may be on its way; if it drops quickly, then rain and wind could be coming, so I'll be extra sure to hold on to the umbrella tightly.

The barograph and barometer were just the beginning. Thermometers and hygrometers (which measure the humidity in the air) were soon ordered. I put a rain gauge out in the

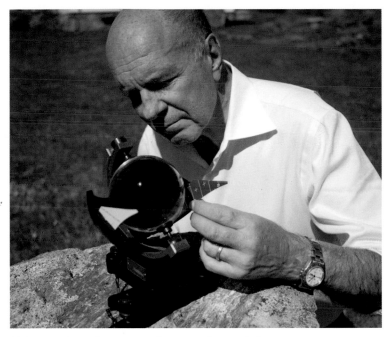

Taking readings from my sunshine recorder is a daily activity.

orchard, and I try to remember to empty its measuring tube each time there has been a rainstorm. (In late March 2010 I recorded well over three inches of rain after a particularly ferocious downpour.)

I also had a firm in London send me a sunshine recorder. This is a wonderful-looking and wickedly primitive device. Basically, it's a large crystal ball with a brass mounting that holds a waterproof recording paper that needs to be changed each morning (therefore requiring seven times more looking after than the once-weekly barograph paper). The sunshine recorder's glass sphere concentrates sunlight onto the paper, where it burns a trace; at the day's end I unclip the paper and have a record—a charred black line, thicker when the sun was intense, nonexistent when clouds swept in—showing me on paper what this one aspect of the day's weather had been like.

To add to all this, I finally bought one specially tuned radio, a device preset to pick up only broadcasts from the National Oceanic and Atmospheric Administration (NOAA). NOAA is the government agency that monitors the weather, provides regular forecasts, and puts out warnings of any menacing storms that may be on their way to a given location, such as my little hilltop farm. Once in a while—usually in the middle of dinner, it seems—a NOAA radio alarm sounds, and a somber automated voice announces that a dangerous thunderstorm will soon arrive—though "damaging winds and rain, heavy at times, lightning strikes, and possible golf-ball-size hail, together with wind gusts in excess of fifty miles an hour" is usually as bad as it gets in this generally rather peaceable corner of the world.

Thus, armed with my cow weather vane and my brass barograph and wooden barometer, along with my thermometers, hygrometers, rain gauge, sunshine recorder, and forecast radio, I maintain a keen amateur's interest in the daily details of my local weather. And all this fascination, all the pleasure I take from the fixed routine of checking my meteorological instruments, was born of that brief moment of editorial disappointment ten years ago, which of course I now realize turned out to be an ill wind (atmospheric phenomenon again!) that *did* blow some good. For now I know, and continue to learn, more about the myriad complexities of the big picture—our climate—and the little picture—our weather.

And there can hardly be a more dramatic demonstration of weather—and indeed, of the climate more generally—than when you get caught in a big Atlantic Ocean hurricane, as thousands in the American northeast did around Halloween in 2012.

THE BIGGEST, BADDEST WEATHER

My experience of Hurricane Sandy—or Frankenstorm, the Blizzacane, the Snor'eastercane, or any of the other outlandish names the press chose to give to the most devastating American weather event of 2012—confirmed what I knew as a homegrown weatherman: when trouble is in the offing, listen very carefully to the weather forecast.

We had been living in a basement apartment in New York City that had flooded once before, so the likelihood of a major storm surge in lower Manhattan was alarming, to say the least. This alarm was reinforced by a passage from one of my recent books. My own words suggested that something terribly bad was about to happen:

> New York sits on stable geological features that rise well above sea level, but it has been tunneled into and bored through until it resembles an ants' nest, and all its tunnels lie well below sea level. A storm surge coming into New York Harbor could flood the subway lines without difficulty. But far more goes on underground than subways: the telecommunications cables and fiber-optic lines alone are vital for the running of the world's financial industries: soak them in the water, and the world starts to fall apart.
>
> Vulnerable cities are not merely going to slide slowly and elegantly under the sea, millimeter by millimeter. They are going to perch on the edge of inundation until a storm rages itself into an uncontrollable maelstrom of fury, and a battering of huge waves breaches the dykes and the levees, and water courses into the city center in torrents, destroying all before it.

Lower Manhattan went dark after that part of New York City lost power due to Hurricane Sandy, 2012.

By Thursday, October 25, 2012, all the computer forecasting models locked themselves into harmony. The predictions became more and more accurate, and the realization more and more acute: a giant storm would actually hit the hinterlands of New York City.

So we got out of town . . . and Sandy roared in.

HURRICANE, THE NAME by which this unimaginably huge and destructive weather system has been known in North America for the last three centuries, comes from the Carib word *huracán,* meaning a "great wind." In other parts of the world, these terrifying, majestic storms are called *cyclones* or *typhoons,* depending upon whether they circulate in a clockwise direction (as they do in the southern hemisphere) or in the opposite (counterclockwise) direction (in the northern hemisphere). *Cyclone* comes from the Greek κυκλῶν, *kyklon,* which translates to "whirling around in a circle"; *typhoon* comes from the Chinese words for "big wind."

Hurricane. Cyclone. Typhoon. What exactly are such giant

The Great Storm of 1815 that hit New England is believed to have been a Category 4 hurricane. Witnesses reported that sea spray made the rain "taste like salt." (For more on hurricane categories, see page 60.)

storms? When, where, and how do they form? And why do such destructive forces even exist? To answer all these questions—an ongoing process, since weather science is an eternally evolving branch of knowledge—requires some very basic understanding of the Earth and the laws of physics that enfold it.

Though they may generate many headlines, hurricanes, cyclones, and typhoons are in fact rather rare events. (For simplicity, I'll just use the word *hurricane* from now on to include all these violent weather monsters.) Only about ninety-six such storms occur every year; roughly a dozen are even named. Most days in the world's tropics, where these storms begin, are pleasing and peaceful; the chances of being affected by a hurricane are quite small. But when the big storms do develop, they can be terrifying, and for centuries they were every bit as mysterious as earthquakes and volcanoes.

As with so many of the world's violent phenomena, hurricanes were long believed to be an act of God. Up until the nineteenth century, no one had any real idea of what these storms were. They arrived from the sea, where they probably had formed, and they soaked and destroyed whatever they passed over on land, then moved on, leaving behind misery and mystery.

But in 1821 a Connecticut saddlemaker and part-time weatherman named William Redfield noticed something: the way trees had been felled by a huge storm that had just passed across his state differed significantly depending on where the trees were. Trees in the eastern corner of Connecticut, where the storm had first swept in from the Atlantic, had all fallen toward the northwest; but the trees in the far west of the state, where Connecticut meets New York, had fallen in a southeasterly direction. The astute Mr. Redfield surmised from this that the storm must have been a

William Redfield.

giant whirlwind—which is, of course, perfectly right.

The diameter of a storm whirlwind was easy enough to establish, so long as observers on the ground took measurements. All they had to do was station human recorders in many parts of the region who, after the storm had swept by, could compare notes about the times the winds had begun to blow and when they abated. The most distant places where winds were blowing at the same time would be, approximately, the edges of the storm's whirlwind: the distance between them, its diameter. If, for example, the wind was found to have been raging in Boston, Massachusetts, at the same time it was blowing hard in Albany, New York, but then the storm cleared Boston but still raged in Albany, one could compute the as-the-crow-flies distance between Boston and Albany—over 150 miles (240 kilometers)—as the probable diameter of the whirlwind.

But how thick were the winds of giant storms? How far up into the atmosphere did they blow? This particular matter took a while to settle. Some observers noted that hurricanes tended to blow themselves out when they met mountain ranges, even low ones. The observers then reasonably drew the conclusion that hurricanes were thin, fragile, ground-hugging, pancake-like structures. Others disputed this, saying that the clouds seen in a hurricane were often of the so-called cirrus variety: tufty-looking (*cirrus* is Latin for "tuft") high-altitude clouds that contain ice crystals and so require great height for survival. To these observers, the shape of a giant storm was much thicker—more cake than pancake. And that was what turned out to be the case, though cake vs. pancake was not decisively

An insignia of US Navy Hurricane Hunters.

proved until the 1930s, when hurricanes were seen from passing aircraft and their approximate thicknesses were measured. Once it had been, then the basic shape of a hurricane was confirmed: it was a spinning high-energy whirlwind full of clouds and lightning, often scores (in some cases hundreds) of miles across, and as many as ten miles (sixteen kilometers) thick.

This whirling mass of clouds—with layers of ice-filled cirrus forming a frosting at the top, then thousands of feet of a creamlike cumulonimbus mousse of thunderclouds in the middle, all sparking with lightning and rich with rain and hail and snowflakes—turns around a central pole that is cloud free and strangely still. This is the fabled *eye* of the hurricane, the place where everything about the storm is so concentrated that there is actually, and ironically, nothing apparently there.

The existence of a hurricane's eye was also not properly known, and its structure not fully understood, until the 1940s, when dedicated hurricane-hunting aircraft were invented. These aircraft were able to pass over a storm and examine the details of its makeup (twenty years later, weather satellites followed). The planes, flown by exceptionally courageous and competent pilots, carried cameras that were parachuted into the eye of the hurricane to capture photographs of the storm's interior.

THE UNITED STATES is the only country with a full-time squadron of aircraft specifically designated as hurricane hunters. It actually has two of them: one is a military squadron operated by the US Air Force (USAF) Reserve, and flying out of an air base in Biloxi, Mississippi; the other, with aircraft filled with sophisticated measuring instruments and crewed by trained civilian meteorologists, is run by NOAA and operates out of a base near Tampa, Florida.

The history of hurricane hunting goes back to World War II (1939–1945). The first plane deliberately flown into a gathering hurricane was sent out by the USAF on a secret pilot-training mission near Galveston, Texas, in 1943. The value of the information gathered by the plane's crew became obvious from the start: they could tell the strength, direction, and general appearance of the storm with far better accuracy than even the best of radars then available.

A variety of aircraft has since been employed over the years—converted bombers, long-range passenger aircraft, and even high-altitude spy planes. These days the USAF uses the Lockheed WC-130J Super Hercules, a modified version of the venerable workhorse transport aircraft, the C-130 Hercules; the USAF hurricane-hunting squadron has thirty-two planes with forty-six more on order, as of this writing. The much smaller NOAA fleet uses Lockheed aircraft as well, but they fly a long-range spotter aircraft called the P-3 Orion, with a Gulf Stream jet for high-altitude observation.

Hurricane-hunting duties are not without risks: since 1945 six aircrews have been lost while flying into cyclonic storms, and even today, with accumulated skills and stronger and more advanced aircraft, crews who dive to five hundred feet (one hundred fifty meters) above sea level and deliberately fly through the eye wall of a monster storm are taking serious chances. It is not a job for the faint of heart.

These days satellites augment—but have not yet replaced—hurricane-hunting crews. Still, there must be a gathering feeling

On July 27, 1943, US Air Force Colonel Joseph Duckworth flew this AT-6 Texan through the eye of a hurricane.

NOAA WP-3D Orions (P-3s).

USAF WC-130J "Hurricane Hunter."

among their number that their highly dangerous, but intensely romantic, calling may not survive for much longer. The accuracy and precision of satellite coverage, and the speed with which these instruments beam pictures down to Earth, may make the idea of sending fragile human beings out into the wild winds and waters far above the oceans seem like an unwise use of taxpayer-funded resources.

The eye and eye wall of a hurricane, photographed from a National Oceanic and Atmospheric Administration (NOAA) P-3 Hurricane Hunter aircraft . . .

. . . and from the International Space Station.

Before the advent of these technologies, the overhead passage of a hurricane eye was, for anyone on the ground, a truly bewildering experience: spectacular, magnificent, and terrifying all at once.

There was no warning, except that the storm became more and more fierce, the rainbands lashed in ever-increasing intensity, the winds rose to a high-pitched banshee howl—until suddenly everything stopped, like the music in musical chairs. The rain ceased, the wind dropped, the crashing and breaking sounds faded, a mysterious stillness draped over the landscape. Far above, a watery sun illuminated great towers of white cloud that rose high into the sky on every side, blocking every possible horizon. Sometimes people saw showers of ice crystals pouring down the sides of the cloud cliffs, which shimmered and glittered as the sun lit the freezing cascades. The crags of rain clouds then formed a protective circular wall, an amphitheater thousands of feet high, a kind of sanctuary. All seemed calm within. People emerged from their shelters to inspect the wreckage—in the mistaken belief that the worst was over.

A very mistaken belief indeed.

Suddenly, and with a deafening new roar, the giant storm raged again: the clouds swiftly turned black and immediately obliterated the sun; the rains started drumming on roofs—and the winds, the winds! They changed within seconds from silent nothing to supergale-force howling, and were soon roaring full tilt, but in *the opposite direction* from the way they had been blowing just minutes before. Trees weakened by powerful winds and now twisted from the other

USAF Hurricane Hunters prepare a dropsonde for launch.

side began to splinter and fall. Roofs were lifted from their moorings, windows were blown in, and people who had so wrongly thought the storm done with were caught unaware and hurt—or killed—by the sudden return of the monster. This, the moment of the passing of the trailing eye wall, is perhaps the most dangerous moment in any hurricane.

Seen from above, in the comfort of an aircraft or from higher still, via the silent remoteness of a weather satellite in space, a hurricane's eye over the sea is benign-looking: a slow, swirling emptiness at the deep center of the storm, the pin in the pinwheel. Examined closely, the eye itself is a little more complicated: the funnel looks rather like the swirl above the drain of a kitchen sink, a gray wash of the sea visible at its very bottom. The roughness of the visible water helped early hurricane-hunter aircraft crews guess the speed of the eye wall winds.

Modern technology allows for an even closer study of the inner workings of a hurricane (and here again, I must stress that what is true for a hurricane, an American and Caribbean storm blowing in a counterclockwise direction, is also true for a Northwest Pacific typhoon and for a southern hemisphere cyclone, even though the winds and spirals of these giant storms track in the opposite, clockwise direction). What the new radars, radio-scattering equipment, and dropsondes (a dropsonde is a clutch of instruments dropped into the eye with a parachute, and which transmits data until it is destroyed by the storm) show is that just outside the eye wall is a rain-free ring that has been called the moat; and beyond that there are spiral bands of highly intense rain. The instruments also showed something unexpected: high above the counterclockwise spiral that is the storm proper, there is a faint pattern of spiraling high-altitude clouds that move in

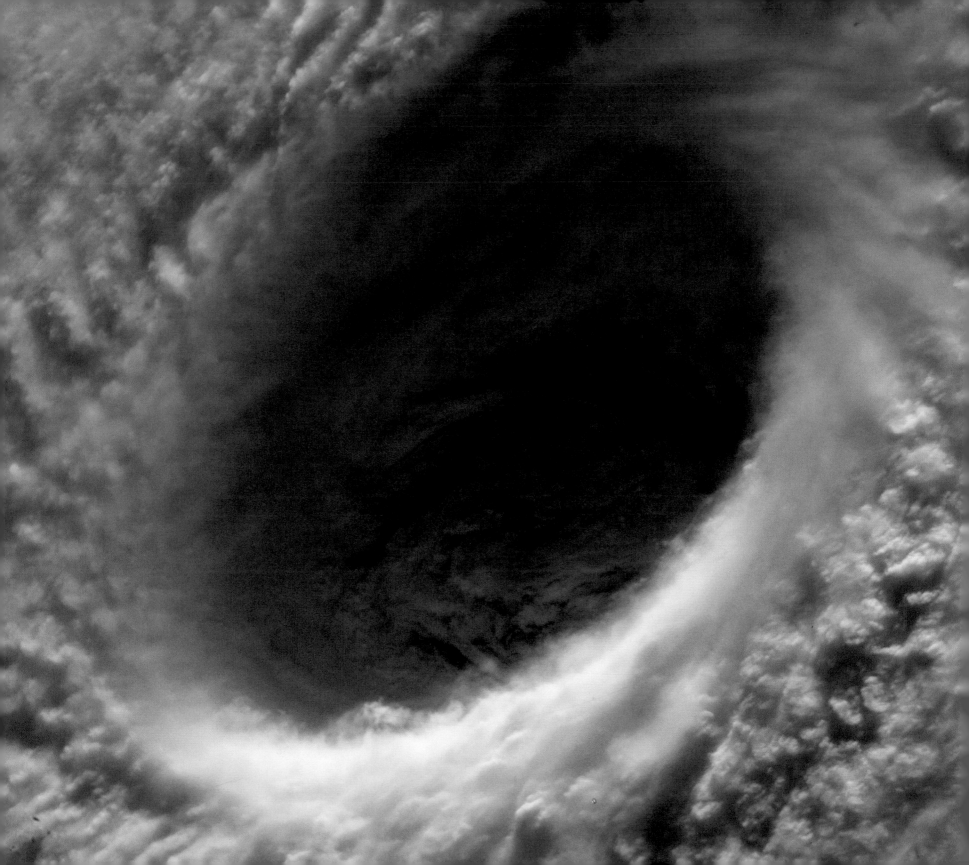

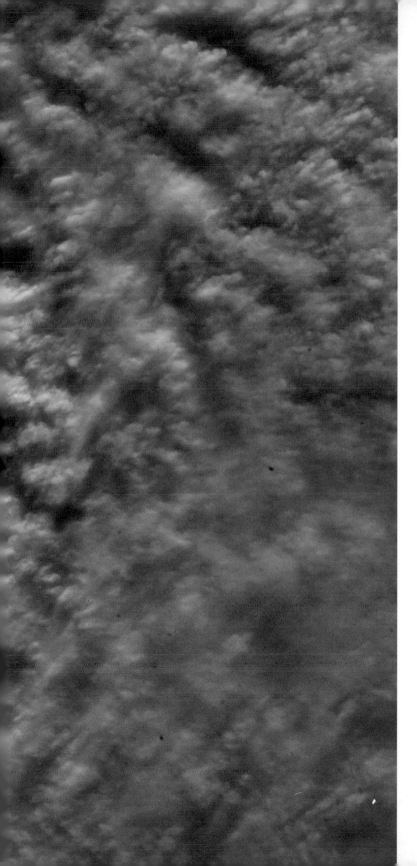

the *opposite* direction. These clouds are not ice-cold as might be expected, but really quite warm.

And therein lies a clue to the beautiful architecture of a fully formed hurricane. For it turns out that, yes, while ice crystals are to be seen cascading down the sides of the eye wall toward the sea below, the main thrust of air inside the central hole that is the eye of the hurricane is not downward but upward. The intensely low pressure that is to be found around a hurricane's center acts like a gigantic suction machine on the ocean, a mile-wide vacuum cleaner that sucks the warm, wet seaside air from above the ocean upward into its own storm center, and then spits it out into the high upper atmosphere, which (because it is relatively cool) condenses the moisture and feeds the hurricane with yet more ice and hail and rain to dump violently onto the ground below.

This enormous weather phenomenon is a thick cream cake of clouds, miles wide, that moves as a whole across the surface of the ocean. Most of it rotates one way, but there is some faint and not-well-organized rotation at the top of the storm in the other direction, plus more ragged and less visible layers of thin high clouds as a demonstration of this counter-rotation.

If the water temperature beneath the storm is warm, then that seawater is sucked up inside the coliseum of storm clouds where the storm center is warm too, and can hold more water than if it were cooler. But once this vacuumed-up water hits the higher altitudes, it cools, dumping this water into yet more clouds, more rain, and more violence. And, generally speaking, considering the direction that most of these giant hurricanes like to take, warm seawater is something they encounter in vast abundance—with the result that the storms become very big and very strong, very quickly.

And very dangerous, to boot.

Eye of Typhoon Maysak (2015).

LIKE MOST GREAT and calamitous events of nature, Hurricane Sandy was a curiously short-lived thing. For most of the three weeks of its existence, it did no harm at all. It was no more than a ripple of high clouds in its early days, and a gusty cluster of cold rainstorms at its end. But at the midperiod of its life, and for six devastating days on and around Halloween 2012, it grew into an absolute and unforgiving monster. It howled with uncontrollable fury, spinning counterclockwise in a 400-mile-wide (644-kilometer-wide) spiral of violence that whiplashed the American Northeast with a brute ferocity seldom experienced.

Although Sandy will be forever remembered as a quintessentially American storm—it did nearly twenty billion dollars' worth of property damage to New York City alone when it struck on the night of October 29, 2012—it was actually born far away from the Americas, off the coast of the Sahara Desert in West Africa.

Sandy's early biography is simple enough. That first unusual ripple of atmospheric activity was noticed by vigilant forecasters around the world on October 11, 2012, in the sea off Mauritania. Unusual, but not alarmingly so: about sixty such ripples occur each year, and almost none

Sandy, the tenth hurricane of the 2012 hurricane season, was given a female name because the storms before and after it (Rafael and Tony) had male names, all in accordance with the Atlantic storm-naming rules of the World Meteorological Organization (WMO). Male and female names alternate on the WMO's six lists of names. The alphabetical lists are rotated every year.

turn into storms. But this one did. The many satellites that tracked it first recorded its presence as a late-season tropical wave—bigger than a ripple and much better organized—when it had taken up residence in the eastern Caribbean on Thursday, October 18. Three days after that, a team of forecasters in Reading, a city in southern England, spotted unmistakable signs that to them—and to them alone, at first—indicated grave danger. Puzzlement reigned. The Reading forecasters still weren't absolutely certain, and their verdict wasn't echoed by other weather offices around the world. The American weather offices in particular were confident that Sandy would head into the central Atlantic Ocean and peter out there quite harmlessly, at most causing big waves for just a scattering of merchant ships at sea. Only the scientists hunched over their terminals in England maintained their conviction that the low-pressure swirling maelstrom of cloud and rain and wind would hit the United States. On Wednesday, October 24, some of these British weather analysts issued warnings that the storm, now gathering in size and strength in a manner rarely seen before, was likely to dive-bomb the states of the American Northeast.

Sandy hit Jamaica as a Category 1 storm on Wednesday, October 24, 2012. Leaving behind a fair amount of repairable damage in Kingston, she churned on northward across the sea, giving earthquake-battered Haiti a stinging wallop as she did so and strengthening all the while, until she hit the eastern tip of the island of Cuba with the hammerblows of a Category 3 hurricane.

Just twenty-four hours later, on Thursday, October 25, the Reading forecasters were proved right: all the computer models from the other forecasting centers, most notably from the machines at the National Hurricane Center in Florida, for some reason suddenly came together. Now there seemed no doubt about it: in three days' time a giant storm would indeed hit the US coastal mainland, somewhere between Washington, D.C., and Boston, Massachusetts. Moreover, Sandy was becoming an unprecedentedly enormous and powerful superstorm.

Forecasts now showed Sandy colliding head on, not just with the American northeast coast, but with a powerful blast of winter weather that was barreling its way down from Canada. At the very same time that Sandy started to edge westward, rigid folds of Arctic air gathered and combined, buffeting the Appalachian Mountains. Clouds heavy with snow and ice and hail and bitter rain headed down toward the ocean to meet the fast-moving hurricane, which was likely to push the sea onshore and make the tides rise way above their normal level. (Not to mention that there was a full moon, which also helped make the tides as much as 20 percent higher.) There would be a truly massive storm surge.

And all this was about to happen over densely populated coastal areas, including one of the most important cities in the world.

The next day, Friday, October 25, even though the weather outside remained balmy around New York City, the official warnings went up. The Bahamas were being knocked about—sixty-seven people died across the Caribbean—and the US government announced that everyone along the East Coast from Virginia to Massachusetts should now acquire an emergency kit of food (including for pets), water, batteries, and flashlights. Virginia, Maryland, and Pennsylvania declared states of emergency, warning that power outages could last days. New York City's mayor told those living in coastal areas of the city—and New York City is almost all coastal, being a port and a harbor and a seaside community—that they should prepare to get going. Nothing mandatory, not yet: just listen to the forecasts, he said, and be prepared. But it soon got worse.

By Saturday, October 26, New Jersey formally ordered people to move away from the coasts. NOAA issued as strongly worded a warning as New Yorkers had ever read.

Warnings kept coming over the weekend: transit systems might close; airports could be shut down; schools could be forced to shutter for days; and the stock market might not open. Cruise ships and naval vessels already in port made steam and put out to sea, where they would be safe from crashing into docksides. Everything depended on whether Sandy would indeed turn inland. On Sunday night the giant storm was still wallowing hugely northeastward, a discus of spiraling clouds spreading hundreds of miles from its eye. It was now three hundred miles (about five hundred kilometers) away from the great lighthouse on Cape Hatteras, North Carolina. But there still seemed a smidgen of a chance that the storm would head straight on and pass harmlessly by.

But then Sandy started to turn.

As Sunday night bled into Monday morning, the now-gigantic weather system moved toward the American coast, just as those canny forecasters in Reading had predicted more than a week before. (The fact that the Europeans got it so right, so quickly, caused a major post-storm uproar in the US Congress, eventually forcing millions of dollars to be spent upgrading America's weather computers.)

Sandy's turn triggered evacuation notices. In New York City, 375,000 residents of those low-lying coastal areas designated as Zone A—the very edges of Manhattan, vulnerable parts of Brooklyn, Queens, and Staten Island—were told to leave. No questions asked. The National Weather Service (NWS) put it bluntly: *Think about your loved ones, think about the emergency responders who will be unable to reach you when you make the panicked phone call to be rescued[;] think about the rescue/recovery teams who will rescue you if you are injured or recover your remains if you do not survive.* At a White House press conference, President Barack Obama was equally clear: "Please listen to what your state and local officials are saying. When they tell you to evacuate, you need to evacuate."

At eight p.m., October 29, 2012, Sandy hit. She came

ashore close to Atlantic City, New Jersey, bringing brutal gale-force winds, pounding rain, and rising tides; the destruction was far more savage than anyone had prepared for.

Sandy devoured her way across New Jersey in monstrous fashion. Icons of the famous Jersey Shore were smashed or flooded: boardwalks were ripped up and scattered, amusement piers thrown into the raging surf, and roller coasters crushed into bundles of twisted iron. Beach houses were up-ended and torn from their foundations—in all, more than 500 were totally wrecked; 72,000 homes were badly damaged and rendered uninhabitable.

The power went out. One by one, substations were overwhelmed by seawater; trees crashed onto transmission lines; gigantic short-circuits arced and burned until by dawn on

Tuesday, two and a half million residents in New Jersey had no electricity.

But if New Jersey suffered badly, New York was battered beyond belief. Rain and wind and explosions in power stations there did fearsome damage. The electricity went out in huge chunks of the city, hundreds of blocks at a time. As harbinger of what was to come, the storm surge flowed over Liberty Island in New York Harbor and the Statue of Liberty's famous light went out. A New York University hospital closed its doors to new arrivals, and then when its backup generators failed, hospital and rescue workers evacuated patients floor by floor through darkened stairwells, carrying some patients on gurneys.

The 90-mile-per-hour (145-kilometer-per-hour) gales

Coastal New York City and the Jersey Shore: what was left after Sandy blew through. Despite the awe-inspiring power of the storm, in technical terms, Sandy wasn't a true hurricane when it hit on October 29. Out at sea, it had been, for sure; but as it made its infamous turn to the west, it lost some of its oomph. When it hit Atlantic City, it was downgraded, classified as a tropical storm.

Flooded subway stop, lower Manhattan.

Breezy Point, the battered tip of New York City's Rockaway peninsula.

were relentless. A crane, high up on the side of a new Midtown skyscraper being built for the world's wealthiest, toppled over in the gathering winds and, during the storm's peak, hung precariously on the building's flanks. The lighthouse keeper at Montauk Point on the far tip of New York's Long Island said the lighthouse shuddered in the storm despite having walls six feet (about two meters) thick; she had been on the station for twenty-six years and had never experienced winds so ferocious.

Water poured into the city from the widely feared storm surge. Manhattan stands at the upper end of a funnel-shaped bay. Sandy relentlessly pushed and sucked billions of tons of full-moon high-tide seawater into this bay, dealing the city a succession of near-lethal blows. The angle of approach and sheer strength of the storm lifted the water nearly fourteen feet (four meters) above normal. Waves more than thirty-two feet (ten meters) high raged through New York Harbor. Huge pounding masses of water roared over the seawalls at the southern end of Manhattan into the Battery, where the tourist boats are moored. The water poured into the open mouths of any low-lying construction it could find. It poured into the Brooklyn–Battery Tunnel. It poured into the mouth of the Holland Tunnel. And, most ominous of all, it poured into the wide throat of the subway station at South Ferry: down the escalators, down through the ticket hall, down past the turnstiles and across the tiled floors and down more steps and stairways, and onto the electric tracks themselves. The New York subway system, a lifeline for millions, was flooding. It was, declared the subway system's chairman, the worst disaster in the system's 108-year history.

All bridges and tunnels into New York City were shut down, effectively cutting Manhattan and Staten Island off from the rest of the world. The New York Stock Exchange announced it would close for two days, longer than ever before. Reports of deaths from falling trees, drowning, and exposure began to trickle in. And still the power kept being cut off: more and more sections of the city went dark, the tallest buildings standing black against a near-black sky, deprived

The southern New Jersey coastline before (August 2012)
and after (November 2012) Sandy.

of even their blinking aircraft-warning beacons. People huddled at their windows, mesmerized by the vision of urban helplessness, a city of millions brought to its knees by a singular, vast, and nearly unprecedented weather event. Later they would remember oddities of the storm: wild rains for ten minutes followed by silence; a full moon shining vaguely through breaks in the clouds; then ferocious gusts of winds and more drenching; warm winds from the ocean, swept away by gusts of cold, snow-laden, sodden air from the north.

The cycles of warm, wet, cold, windy, moonlit, warm, wet, cold, windy, moonlit, warm . . . repeated themselves over and over through the night and into the next terrible, blustery, wet, powerless, strange gray day. Dawn broke on

Tuesday, October 30, to display roads covered with broken trees or deep with water. Cars were floating about randomly. Sirens were blaring. Fires had broken out. A boat, carried inland by the rogue waters, lay fully across a railroad line. National Guard troops, ordered into the city by New York State's governor, were patrolling, in uniform, no guns.

And what of the mail carriers and their famous (though unofficial) motto that "neither snow nor rain nor heat nor gloom of night stays these couriers from the swift completion of their appointed rounds"? Mail service in and around New York was canceled, or "curtailed" as the government later put it. Sandy, it seemed, had trumped everything.

By the morning of Halloween—the public celebration of which was officially canceled in both New York and New Jersey, along with the New York City Marathon, scheduled for the following weekend—Superstorm Sandy had finally left, blowing across the Allegheny Mountains to go cause trouble in the Ohio Valley and the Great Lakes. New York, New Jersey, and other points along the East Coast were drying out, digging out, staggering back to life, and counting the cost.

And the cost was indeed horrendous. Two hundred thirty-three people died directly or indirectly in consequence of the storm, thirty-seven of them in New Jersey, where Sandy first made landfall. Fifty-three New Yorkers died; 600,000 people there lost power; 100,000 homes were severely damaged. Fires destroyed 100 of the homes; 250,000 vehicles were damaged. Gasoline supplies were cut to almost nil, and long lines sprang up as far away as northern New Jersey. The total cost to New York City was 19 billion dollars. And overall Sandy's effects were stunning: with the dead, the injured, and the wreckage all around, and costs of as much as 68 billion dollars, it was the second most tragically expensive Atlantic storm after Hurricane Katrina in 2005 (see page 32).

JUST WHY DOES a hurricane spin in a counterclockwise direction, and its southern colleague, the cyclone, spin in the opposite direction? The short answer: a hurricane spins because the Earth rotates.

We all agree that our planet rotates around its vertical axis and makes a complete circle once a day. The speed at which it moves, however, varies according to where you are on the planet's surface. The circumference of the Earth at the equator, where the Earth is fattest, is about 24,900 miles (40,000 kilometers). A flag placed at the equator will cover that distance in one rotation, in one day. But a flag placed somewhere in the north of Canada, where the Earth is a lot narrower, might travel only 2,400 miles (3,900 kilometers) in one rotation in that same one day, because the Earth's circumference is many fewer miles there. So in terms of miles per hour, with the day having twenty-four hours in it, it is fair to say the equator is moving at a little more than 1,000 miles (1,600 kilometers) per hour, while subarctic Canada is only chugging along at a little more than 300 miles (500 kilometers) per hour. (The same would be true if we had placed our flag down near Antarctica.) So Earth's northernmost or southernmost places rotate at a much slower rate than the world's spin at the equator.

Now, suppose you had superhuman strength and could hurl a ball from a spot on the fast-moving equator due north toward that spot in subarctic Canada. Remember, you're on the equator, flying along at a bit over 1,000 miles (1,600 kilometers) per hour, but as the ball flew farther and farther north, the Earth below it would be passing by more and more slowly. When the ball finally fell to Earth, it would do so not where you had aimed it, but at a point considerably to the right of where you had intended it to go. So on a map, the ball would seem to describe a curved path rather than a straight line, and it would be deflected to the east. It is this

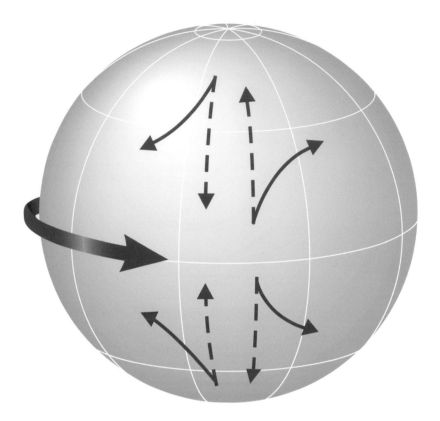

The deflections in this diagram show the Coriolis effect.

deflection that sets storms rotating. Remember there is a near-vacuum, an eye, in a storm's center. The air around the eye rushes to fill it.

Nature abhors a vacuum. It likes to bring things into equilibrium. So if there is a big storm forming in the northern hemisphere the surrounding air and all the elements carried by it—clouds, ice crystals, rain globules, hailstones, snow—will try to rush in toward the vacuum-like eye. But thanks to the curving-to-the-right deflection caused by the differing speeds of the rotation of the earth, the rushing elements won't reach the eye directly. Instead they'll be knocked slightly off course and to the right. And this causes the whole apparatus of the storm to begin spiraling in a counterclockwise direction. The force of the deflection is known as the Coriolis effect, after the nineteenth-century French mathematician-engineer-scientist Gaspard-Gustave de Coriolis, who studied the transfer of energy in rotating systems.

Remember, in the northern hemisphere, the moving air curves to the right. In the southern hemisphere, the opposite is true. Here a curving-to-the-left deflection operates for exactly the same reason. The winds of a southern hemisphere storm, heading in toward the low-pressure zone in the storm center, would all be nudged slightly leftward, making the whole structure of storm clouds and violent rain spin in a clockwise direction.

Hurricanes, when we use the term specifically and in contrast to cyclones and typhoons, are in nearly all cases phenomena peculiar to the North American continent. There are certainly Pacific-originating hurricanes, which tend to be born in the waters off the west coast of Mexico and head westward out across the Pacific Ocean. Some of them curve backward and strike the coast of California. But this pattern is not very common. The more numerous and famous—or infamous, given the havoc they wreak—Atlantic hurricanes are generally born in the eastern Atlantic Ocean. They track westward and then usually northward, hitting home either on the Caribbean islands or on the east, southern, or southeastern coasts of the United States.

When Atlantic hurricanes blow in from the ocean, they can hit the US shorelines in a swath of country that stretches from the Gulf of Mexico to the low-lying barrier islands off the Carolinas. Occasionally, they are to be encountered farther north, affecting Virginia, Maryland, Delaware, New Jersey, New York, and, in some extreme cases, the coastal states of New England. But the places most commonly affected tend to be in Texas, Louisiana, Mississippi, Alabama, and Florida—Florida most notably—together with Georgia and North and South Carolina. Bad weather—or worse, trails of wreckage—are commonplace for these states during hurricane season, which runs from June to November.

Hurricanes are part and parcel of a coastal way of life for millions of Americans.

That makes the answers to questions about where these storms travel and whether it is possible to forecast where they are likely to go extremely important. Statistical records of past storms paint a portrait of their most common tracks; the study of the atmosphere offers the reasons they move as they do; and examples from the past demonstrate what can happen when someone gets the forecast wrong.

The Deadliest US Hurricanes	Year	Category	Deaths
1. Great Galveston Hurricane (Texas)	1900	4	8,000
2. Lake Okeechobee (Florida)	1928	4	2,500
3. Katrina (Louisiana, Mississippi, Florida, Georgia, Alabama)	2005	3	1,200
4. Cheniere Caminada (Louisiana)	1893	4	1,100–1,400
5. Sea Islands (South Carolina, Georgia)	1893	3	1,000–2,000
6. Georgia, South Carolina	1881	2	700
7. Audrey (Southwest Louisiana, North Texas)	1957	4	416
8. Great Labor Day Hurricane (Florida Keys)	1935	5	408
9. Last Island (Louisiana)	1856	4	400
10. Miami Hurricane (Florida, Mississippi, Alabama)	1926	4	372

As I've noted already, most Atlantic hurricanes typically begin to grow in the eastern part of the ocean, close to the western coast of Africa. These fledgling storms usually head westward in a more or less straight line. They do so because

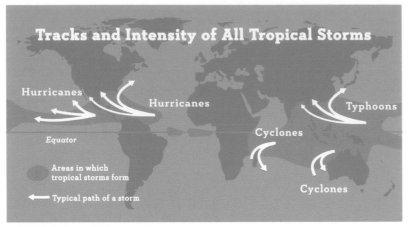

A *NASA* chart of where monster storms occur.

they are steered westward by the northeast trade winds, which blow constantly in the tropics toward the west. (The northeast trades are so named because they blew trading ships across the sea at a reliable twelve knots or so. The winds blew from the northeast, pushing these sailing vessels off to the southwest and to the ports of the New World.)

The trade winds act as a kind of conveyor belt, moving storms westward along with them. When these storms get into the Caribbean, though, something else usually happens. By then a particular storm has become strong enough to create vortices, or masses of swirling air. These vortices have an interesting effect on the passage of the storm.

A typical fast-forming hurricane moving happily along its trade wind conveyor belt picks up intensity as it goes along. Its winds spin around in a counterclockwise direction, pushed to do so by the Coriolis effect. The counterclockwise spinning causes the air on the eastern side of the hurricane to move northward. This air (the air that is not part of the storm but is off to its east) will itself begin to spin . . . but in a clockwise fashion. It will become a vortex, spinning around and eventually moving up to a position to the northeast of the hurricane.

Meanwhile, another vortex will develop to the west of the storm. The hurricane winds there sweep in a southerly direction. This causes the air nearby to start spinning in a counterclockwise direction, creating a new vortex that hovers around the storm on its southwestern side.

The hurricane is now accompanied by two vortices, or what meteorologists call beta gyres. As the storm strengthens, the beta gyres start steering. This force affects the way the hurricane shifts. Usually, the air currents around the beta gyres of a typical hurricane help push the storm off its westerly track and shove it along a more northerly path.

Storm statistics show that almost all Atlantic hurricanes move along in a westerly stream. When they become large enough, they start edging northward and colliding with places on the coasts of Florida and the Carolinas. If the vortices were not there, these hurricanes would all move along in more or less unwavering straight lines and crash directly into Central America or the Yucatán. But they don't: the vortices are why.

All that said, a thousand other ripples and churns in the atmosphere can turn up at apparently random moments and affect the way a storm moves as well. So while the general hurricane path is a shove to the west and then a nudge to the northwest, it isn't always the case. Sometimes, because of unseen and unanticipated happenings in the atmosphere, forecasters can get things terribly wrong . . . with disastrous results.

A serious misreading took place in the United States at the beginning of the last century. A US Weather Bureau meteorologist named Isaac Cline was based in Galveston, Texas. Back then Galveston was a fast-growing city built on a barrier island on the coast south of Houston. Cline was the first government forecaster to be stationed in Texas.

A map of Galveston, Texas, 1885.

Galveston was happy to have him, because this confirmed its inhabitants' view that theirs was the premier city in the state.

Soon after settling in, Cline declared that it was crazy to imagine a major storm ever affecting a town that lay so far from most hurricane tracks. "The opinion held by some . . . that Galveston will at some time be seriously damaged by some such disturbance, is simply an absurd delusion," he told the local paper in 1891. Cline was so certain of this, and the Galveston city fathers were so convinced of Cline's wisdom and prescience, that they decided not to build a seawall around the city, despite petitions from hundreds of residents who lived down by the coast.

In late August 1900, a number of ships and island observatories dotted around the eastern Caribbean began sending in reports of a major tropical storm that was churning through the region. Of course there was no radar in 1900, no spotter planes—no planes at all, in fact. No radio, either. Just dispatches from newly docked ships and a few news reports telegraphed from storm-struck islands. Weather forecasts back then were deeply unreliable, based on relatively little information and a near-total dearth of statistics. To complicate matters, there was an intense rivalry among forecasters. The head office of the US Weather Bureau was wildly disdainful of the forecasters in Cuba, for instance, and cautioned people not to pay any heed to Cuban reports. This went for information from people outside the bureau too, even if they were reporting on what was happening right outside their windows. Only the Weather Bureau specialists in Washington, D.C., and Bureau men out in the field, like Cline in Galveston, truly knew what was going on, what was likely to occur.

Isaac Cline.

Isaac Cline, like his bosses, believed this particular storm in the summer of 1900 would eventually turn to the north. At first he was right. Cline predicted the storm would hit the Caribbean island of Antigua, and it did. It then would (and did) make for the south coast of Hispaniola. It would (and did) nudge itself northward and glance off Cuba; and then it would (and did) turn north and run up toward Florida.

And then Cline's forecasting luck ran out.

He thought the hurricane would next run up the Atlantic side of Florida and hit the US East Coast head on, somewhere to the south of Newport News, Virginia. The hurricane, in Cline's view and that of the forecasters at the Weather Bureau's head office, should have turned up along the Florida coast, sucking up new heat and energy from the warm waters of the Gulf Stream, and then should have thundered its way to the Cape Hatteras lighthouse in North Carolina and to its grim rendezvous with the Virginia beaches.

For a while the storm did turn north. No doubt it was influenced by the vortices mentioned above. But then, unnoticed by everyone, it suddenly did the unthinkable. Pushed by a strange and unseen ripple in the upper atmosphere, and carelessly shrugging off the influence of the vortices beside it, the hurricane turned back on itself just as it passed the tiny islands of Key West, Florida. It never did hit the East Coast; it didn't even get to within a thousand miles of it.

Instead, nudged and pushed and otherwise affected by those strange ripples and unseen airstreams in the upper atmosphere, this ever-growing behemoth barreled clear across the Gulf of Mexico. At dusk on Saturday, September 8, 1900, it slammed head on into the coastal city of Galveston.

There was no seawall.

The city was built on a sandy island, surrounded by sea.

The highest point in town was only about nine feet (three meters) above sea level.

Hurricane winds blasted Galveston at 145 miles (233 kilometers) per hour. The tidal surge was more than fifteen feet (four and a half meters) above normal; it rushed across the city, drowning almost the entire municipal center. What little the seas spared, the gales savagely tore down.

The dead, the survivors, and the devastation in Galveston.

The storm's effects were historic. The damage, devastation, and death toll combined to make the Galveston Hurricane of 1900 the greatest single calamity and natural disaster in all of America's two-and-a-half-century history. Between eight and twelve thousand people perished. Almost all the city's houses were smashed to smithereens or swept out to sea. The bridges to the mainland were destroyed, the telegraph lines broken; no one knew of the plight of the survivors, nor the number of casualties, for many critical hours.

Who was at fault? The Weather Bureau in large part, because its officials in Washington insisted that they, and only they, had the authority to issue storm warnings—and they were terrified of risking economic damage if they turned out to be wrong. While the hurricane was bearing down on this vulnerable, unknowing Texas town, Washington was still warning residents to evacuate coastal communities in New Jersey!

Isaac Cline was part of this system. He later tried to cover up his incompetence, insisting that on the Saturday afternoon before the disaster broke, he ran frantically along the beaches, warning people to take cover. None of the survivors remember his doing so. So Cline's reputation today remains firmly linked, fairly or unfairly, to the tragedy. He was a dreadful forecaster, and his mistakes are still cruelly memorialized: the Galveston Hurricane of 1900 is known as Isaac's Storm.

FORECASTERS THESE DAYS, now armed with much better technology, usually get things right. But not always. One modern example of forecasting that hit home for me, particularly, I shall never forget.

It was the summer of 1995, and I was living in the port city of Hong Kong, off mainland China. One Friday afternoon I turned on the radio and heard an announcement that the Hong Kong Royal Observatory had just hoisted a stand-by signal, typhoon warning Number One. (The observatory still spoke of "hoisting" signals, just as it used to raise flags in the days before radio, to let shipowners know what the weather was doing.) A typhoon had been spotted somewhere near the Philippines, was heading in a roughly northwesterly direction, and had breached the perimeter line of a five-hundred-mile (eight-hundred-kilometer) circle drawn around Hong Kong.

Everyone understood the range of typhoon warnings. Signal Number One meant that a storm had been spotted inside the five-hundred-mile line. Nothing to worry about: just be aware there was a storm at sea somewhere, near enough to be a possible nuisance.

Signal Number Three signified that the cyclone (*typhoon* was more colloquial) was close enough to cause gale-force winds. All loose objects should be secured, all scaffolding tied down, all potted plants removed from balconies.

Signal Number Eight was the bad one: if that was ever hoisted, all business in Hong Kong was compelled to come to an immediate stop. The government shut down, people were told to go home, and buses and subway trains were given four hours' notice to cease operation.

Everyone hoped Signal Number Ten would never be hoisted. That meant a direct hit was coming. The storm would surge into the city harbor itself, roar over the islands and mountain peaks, bury Hong Kong in lashing rain and broken trees, and, most lethal of all, send hundreds of wind-whipped sheets of corrugated metal used throughout the city flying hundreds of feet into the air. A person could be sliced to shreds in seconds.

That Friday night both television and radio stations kept mentioning the fact that the Number One signal was up. Most stores, similarly, had notices in English and Chinese in their windows: TYPHOON SIGNAL NUMBER ONE HAS BEEN HOISTED. BE AWARE. BE PREPARED. Some of the fancier stores had maps with thumbtacks, showing the track of the cyclone as the Royal Observatory put out its hourly notices.

That weekend I noticed the pins were being placed closer and closer together, tracking westward, coming steadily toward Hong Kong's offshore islands. Then palm trees nearby began to move on Saturday evening. A greasy swell rose out in the harbor, setting the boats rolling in their moorings, their halyards pinging against masts with sudden urgency.

Signal Number Three was hoisted on Saturday evening. It began to rain. At about four a.m., the storm suddenly began to wheel itself to the north. I went to bed, greatly relieved—only to be startled awake by the radio alarm at seven a.m., and an excited announcer declaring, "The Number Eight is up. All businesses, shops, schools, government buildings, and courts are to be closed. To repeat: Signal Number Eight is up, and so Hong Kong is officially closed down."

I called the Royal Observatory to ask what was going on. "An abundance of caution," said the man who answered. "We don't want any nasty surprises. It may change course again. We have to be careful."

The storm never did change course. It missed Hong Kong by fifty miles (eighty kilometers).

Many of the city's inhabitants were annoyed by the shut-

A typhoon warning posted in Hong Kong's airport on September 22, 2013, and a chart of the warning signals.

down. The Hong Kong High Court officially declared itself to have been extremely irritated at having to delay its hearings because of what the court suspected was the amateurish incompetence of whoever had acted as chief hoister of storm signals. A court official telephoned the Royal Observatory to complain. The startled weatherman on the other end of the phone was told only to hoist the Number Eight when he absolutely, certainly, really needed to. The Hong Kong High Court's important business could not stop every time there was a rain shower.

Two weeks later another storm barreled toward Hong Kong. The Royal Observatory, now mindful of judicial and public opinion, did not lean toward an "abundance of caution" this time. Yes, when the new storm system passed across the five-hundred-mile territorial line, the Number One signal went up. The signs appeared in the stores; the radio and TV began to remind the six million people in the area that bad weather was on the way. Once the palm trees began to shake and the waves began to crash against the wharves at the Queen's Pier, the Number Three signal followed. But after that, nothing.

Twelve hours later Typhoon Kent slammed into Hong Kong head on, luckily harming no one, but doing millions of dollars of damage and stirring up a discussion of which is better: major warnings issued every time a storm appears on the horizon, or no major warnings at all?

MORE OFTEN THAN not these days, the world's weather services get their forecasts spot-on right. A classic example of the ever-improving forecasting skills came in the late summer of 2005, with the most notorious of all recent American storms.

This storm of August 2005 was the third most lethal hurricane in the nation's history. Because it did so much damage to a fine modern city jam-packed with people and possessions of great worth, it is the most costly storm of all time. This storm was Hurricane Katrina, which killed 1,200 people in and around the city of New Orleans and did damage that present-day estimates say went as high as 180 billion dollars. Katrina was a true monster storm, and the size of the monstrosity was amply and impeccably forecast by one lone, unlikely-to-be-remembered government forecaster named Robert Ricks.

A NASA image of the infamous storm.

The National Weather Service (NWS) is a government body that was created in 1870 "for giving notice . . . of the approach and force of storms." NWS notices rarely display excitement or emotion. Calmly, dispassionately, this government group records the daily doings in the atmosphere and issues its forecasts in direct and staid language. NWS forecasters seldom get carried away with the temper of their language, even for hurricanes and tornadoes.

But on Sunday morning, August 28, 2005, Robert Ricks, working in front of a bank of weather computers in the NWS office in Slidell, Louisiana, realized something dire was about to happen. An almighty monster of a summer storm had New Orleans in its gunsight and was hurtling unerringly toward the city of nearly five hundred thousand inhabitants. The situation as Ricks saw it was frightening enough to forget about tempered language. People needed to take notice of his forecast. His bulletin (right) has since become a legend in world weather forecasting circles:

URGENT—WEATHER MESSAGE

NATIONAL WEATHER SERVICE NEW ORLEANS LA

1011 AM CDT SUN AUG 28, 2005

. . . DEVASTATING DAMAGE EXPECTED . . .

HURRICANE KATRINA . . . A MOST POWERFUL HURRICANE WITH UNPRECEDENTED STRENGTH . . . RIVALING THE INTENSITY OF HUR—RICANE CAMILLE OF 1969.

MOST OF THE AREA WILL BE UNINHABITABLE FOR WEEKS . . . PERHAPS LONGER. AT LEAST ONE HALF OF WELL CONSTRUCTED HOMES WILL HAVE ROOF AND WALL FAILURE. ALL GABLED ROOFS WILL FAIL . . . LEAVING THOSE HOMES SEVERELY DAMAGED OR DESTROYED.

THE MAJORITY OF INDUSTRIAL BUILDINGS WILL BECOME NON FUNCTIONAL. PARTIAL TO COMPLETE WALL AND ROOF FAILURE IS EX—PECTED. ALL WOOD—FRAMED LOW RISING APARTMENT BUILDINGS WILL BE DESTROYED. CONCRETE BLOCK LOW RISE APARTMENTS WILL SUSTAIN MAJOR DAMAGE . . . INCLUDING SOME WALL AND ROOF FAILURE.

HIGH RISE OFFICE AND APARTMENT BUILDINGS WILL SWAY DAN—GEROUSLY . . . A FEW TO THE POINT OF TOTAL COLLAPSE. ALL WINDOWS WILL BLOW OUT.

AIRBORNE DEBRIS WILL BE WIDESPREAD . . . AND MAY INCLUDE HEAVY ITEMS SUCH AS HOUSEHOLD APPLI—ANCES AND EVEN LIGHT VEHICLES. SPORT UTILITY VEHICLES AND LIGHT TRUCKS WILL BE MOVED. THE BLOWN DEBRIS WILL CREATE ADDITIONAL DESTRUCTION. PERSONS . . . PETS . . . AND LIVESTOCK EXPOSED TO THE WINDS WILL FACE CERTAIN DEATH IF STRUCK.

POWER OUTAGES WILL LAST FOR WEEKS . . . AS MOST POWER POLES WILL BE DOWN AND TRANSFORMERS DESTROYED. WATER SHORTAGES WILL MAKE HUMAN SUFFERING INCREDIBLE BY MODERN STANDARDS.

THE VAST MAJORITY OF NATIVE TREES WILL BE SNAPPED OR UPROOTED. ONLY THE HEARTIEST WILL REMAIN STANDING . . . BUT BE TOTALLY DEFOLIATED. FEW CROPS WILL REMAIN. LIVESTOCK LEFT EXPOSED TO THE WINDS WILL BE KILLED.

AN INLAND HURRICANE WIND WARNING IS ISSUED WHEN SUSTAINED WINDS NEAR HURRICANE FORCE . . . OR FREQUENT GUSTS AT OR ABOVE HURRICANE FORCE . . . ARE CERTAIN WITHIN THE NEXT 12 TO 24 HOURS.

ONCE TROPICAL STORM AND HURRICANE FORCE WINDS ONSET . . . DO NOT VENTURE OUTSIDE!

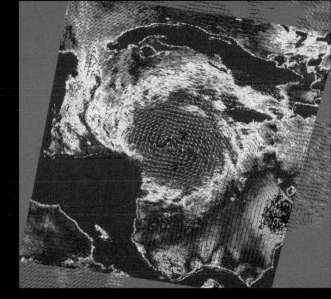

An infrared satellite image of Hurricane Katrina shows the storm's intensity; white is the most intense, followed by red, green, and blue.

Up to thirty thousand people sheltered in the Louisiana Superdome (bottom, center), which lost part of its roof covering during Katrina.

Rescue workers leave their mark; the zero at the bottom of the X indicates no victims or bodies were found.

The people and city of New Orleans were devastated by Katrina, as were places like Waveland, Mississippi. Other areas of Louisiana, Mississippi, Florida, and more than a dozen other US states were affected by the giant storm.

Everything Robert Ricks said that Sunday turned out to be precisely right. Hurricane Katrina, which barreled into the city of New Orleans the very next day, was a truly incredible storm. More than twelve hundred people died; whole townships were ruined; vast regions were evacuated; nearly all the levees that protected the low-lying city were breached, and the resulting floods lasted for months. At least 180 billion dollars in damage was done in and around the much-loved city.

Thousands of frightened, hungry, desperate people were herded into a sports stadium for shelter, a stadium that itself became a nightmare of violence and death. A bewildered government failed for several days to rise to the challenge of the storm, and the losses—to life, to property, to reputation—were staggering.

The deceptively innocent name "Katrina" has since become a byword for many things, alleged government incompetence in dealing with the storm's aftermath being one of them. But above all else, it has since become shorthand for the truly terrifying majesty of unimaginably huge and destructive cyclonic storm systems.

THE NUMEROUS STORMS that form each year, and the dozen or so of these that grow into life-threatening monsters, occur principally in three bands around the world: one band in the tropical northern Atlantic, a second in the tropical northern Pacific, the third in the tropical southern Pacific. They occur at certain times of the year: in the hot months between May and October in the Atlantic, in the hot months between May and October in the Pacific, and in the hot months between November and March in the South Seas.

The two key words associated with cyclonic storm formation are *tropical* and *hot*. It goes without saying that the summertime tropics are always hot. But there are not always storms. Why not?

Think about a car parked quietly out in the street, its tank full of gas. It's always ready to go, but it doesn't run all the time. The car starts only when you trigger it to do so by turning the ignition key. The hot tropics are much the same, always standing by, fully fueled and ready to produce a storm. But they lack the ignition key that makes them suddenly turn on. For a storm to begin, some set of circumstances has to arise in the hot tropics that is the key or trigger—and science has spent a great deal of time in the last half century figuring out what that might be.

Thousands of feet up in the sky directly above the Sahara Desert in North Africa, climatic events give rise to gigantic storms. These events are known as African easterly waves (AEW). They appear to be caused by east-to-west air moving in from the Indian Ocean that then encounters the tremendously hot and dry region of the Sahara below. Surges of heat push the air upward into the cooler high atmosphere. This upflow causes a sudden instability in the atmosphere—its principal feature being an area of low pressure, the upwelling causing a lack of air, a lack of pressure.

Studies have shown that this area of instability is usually bean-shaped and a few hundred miles in length; its long axis points north to south. These bean shapes drift and wobble across the southern Sahara, pushed along by the prevailing easterly winds in these latitudes. A new unstable wave like this appears every three or four days. Eventually a train of these elongated areas of low pressure, with their characteristic high clouds and lightning storms, becomes a common feature of high summer in Sub-Saharan Africa. The phenomenon is visible down below, too. Villagers in Niger, Mali, and Mauritania may spot sudden spurts of winds, tiny gusts, and small whirling dust devils, hints on the ground of what is happening in the skies far above. They may hear the instability in the skies in growls of thunder at night, or see flickers of dry lightning.

Who would have thought that the existence of the Sahara Desert, with its pale and reflective yellow sands and equatorial heat beating down upon it, would cause disturbances in the atmosphere that could in turn cause storms in the Carolinas or Texas or New York? But this is the first indication of a possible hurricane: an AEW heading westward.

The wave crosses to the West African coast and heads out to the sea. It travels at about twenty miles (thirty-two kilometers) per hour, covering nearly five hundred miles (eight hundred kilometers) in a day. At this stage the AEW is a fragile thing, a small cloud meringue in the sky. It is pushed along gently by the steering winds above. If it is pushed too hard, the wave will simply break under the strain, fracturing into a thousand smaller clouds and then vanishing.

Most of these AEWs do break up, but every fourth or fifth one manages to survive the pushing, and glides for long enough to reach the Cape Verde islands, the barren and waterless archipelago of volcanoes off the northwestern coast of Africa. Here, the surviving waves begin to pick up more moisture from the warmer waters of the Atlantic Ocean. Once they do that, they start to assume a form recognizable

Dust blowing westward from the Sahara creates a brownish haze over the Cape Verde islands off the northwest coast of Africa (2002).

on the world's weather radars. Large masses of cumulonimbus thunderclouds rise up to join the disturbance. If these clouds gather in sufficient numbers and combine within the AEW into a slowly strengthening protective envelope of pressure, the assemblage begins to move. Crucially, it then starts to spiral due to the Coriolis effect.

The AEW becomes first a tropical depression; then, if the original low pressure at its center deepens, it becomes a true tropical storm. This assembled formation joins the steering winds, like a vehicle locking its wheels into the track of a car wash. It is pulled and pushed westward, evolving still further as it does so.

In summertime in this part of the Atlantic Ocean, there is a large area of high pressure over the islands of the Azores, west of Portugal, called the Azores High. Languid high-altitude winds circulate around this area in a clockwise fashion. If the newborn tropical storm forms just to the southeast of the Azores High, it will be swept around its southern edge in a westerly direction. Then it will join the trade winds and move steadily and ponderously but firmly toward the western part of the ocean and the Americas.

A remarkable photograph taken from a satellite in late August 1996 shows the North Atlantic Ocean with no fewer than four storms in their respective stages of development, as they are borne westward on these ever-reliable summer trade winds. Off the African coast, above Cape Verde, is a vague swirl of clouds busily transforming itself from an AEW through to a tropical depression and toward a tropical storm. Next, five hundred miles (eight hundred kilometers) to the west, there is a proper, if ragged, formation of swirling clouds, Tropical Storm Gustav. Another eight hundred miles (thirteen hundred kilometers) on, over the Antilles, a fully fledged hurricane named Fran has formed its eye: low pressure intensifying inside it, warm water-soaked air being forced up through the towering eye walls, gales swirling around in a vast spiral of storms; and then, tightly coiled and ready to wreak havoc off the American coast, there is a fourth formation, Hurricane Edouard.

Some cyclonic storms are big, some puny. Some kill thousands; some cause billions of dollars in property loss. Notorious monsters like Katrina, Camille, Andrew, Ike,

A satellite photo taken for the International Satellite Cloud Climatology Project (ISCCP) on August 31, 1996, shows four storms.

Sandy, Hugo, Wilma, Rita, the Galveston Storm of 1900, the Labor Day Hurricane of 1935, and the Okeechobee Hurricane of 1928 were all great Atlantic storms of truly historic, frightening, and destructive proportions.

Fear and destruction are not true storm measurements, however. Nor are financials, another of the most commonly used measurement of storms. In America, Atlantic hurricanes tend to be popularly described by their eventual cost. The Federal Emergency Management Agency (FEMA) quoted damages of 108 billion dollars for Hurricane Katrina, causing it to be seen as the absolute worst storm in US history. But costs are not neutral factors. Storms that strike American cities are expensive because they wreck expensive things. Storms that strike isolated cities in the eastern Philippines may cause just as much devastation, but in dollar terms are much less costly. Human damage, of course, is different—but that's not a neutral measurement either, since a typhoon hitting a crowded slum will kill far more than one that sinks ships and swamps atolls out in the middle of the ocean.

Scales do exist to measure storm intensity, but they are not perfect either. Most, such as the Saffir-Simpson scale, use wind speed as a categorizing tool because wind does the damage and suggests the overall energy—the kinetic energy of a fast-rotating body of air—of the storm as a whole. Critics reasonably complain that ignoring the amount of rainfall or the speed with which the storm develops or the storm surge it creates renders a wind-only classification of somewhat limited use—at least, beyond the news, for which wind speed offers a suitably vivid demonstration of a storm's power.

Saffir-Simpson Scale

Category	Sustained Winds	Types of Damage Due to Hurricane Winds
1	74-95 mph 64-82 kt 119-153 km/h	**Very dangerous winds will produce some damage:** Well-constructed frame homes could have damage to roof, shingles, vinyl siding, and gutters. Large branches of trees will snap and shallowly rooted trees may be toppled. Extensive damage to power lines and poles likely will result in power outages that could last a few to several days.
2	96-110 mph 83-95 kt 154-177 km/h	**Extremely dangerous winds will cause extensive damage:** Well-constructed frame homes could sustain major roof and siding damage. Many shallowly rooted trees will be snapped or uprooted and block numerous roads. Near-total power loss is expected with outages that could last from several days to weeks.
3 (major)	111-129 mph 96-112 kt 178-208 km/h	**Devastating damage will occur:** Well-built framed homes may incur major damage or removal of roof decking and gable ends. Many trees will be snapped or uprooted, blocking numerous roads. Electricity and water will be unavailable for several days to weeks after the storm passes.
4 (major)	130-156 mph 113-136 kt 209-251 km/h	**Catastrophic damage will occur:** Well-built framed homes can sustain severe damage with loss of most of the roof structure and/or some exterior walls. Most trees will be snapped or uprooted and power poles downed. Fallen trees and power poles will isolate residential areas. Power outages will last weeks to possibly months. Most of the area will be uninhabitable for weeks or months.
5 (major)	157 mph or higher 137 kt or higher 252 km/h or higher	**Catastrophic damage will occur:** A high percentage of framed homes will be destroyed, with total roof failure and wall collapse. Fallen trees and power poles will isolate residential areas. Power outages will last for weeks to possibly months. Most of the area will be uninhabitable for weeks or months.

Newscasters aside, the most ideal and neutral way of describing a giant storm is to define the event according to the lowest pressure recorded in the storm's eye. The lower the minimum central pressure, the more intense the storm.

Gauging a storm's minimum central pressure was difficult in the era before satellites and storm-hunting aircraft. Even nowadays, a dropsonde needs to be inserted into the eye of the hurricane to obtain this information. Measuring by minimum central pressure makes the records of storms more useful. It becomes possible to compare one ocean's violence with another and a given year's storms against another time period to help spot climatic trends.

This measurement of pressure has an impact on the hurricane classification tables. What seem to be the biggest and costliest storms often come behind the storms with lower central pressure. And if you measure this way, most Atlantic hurricanes come second in terms of power to those cyclones and typhoons that regularly cannonade across the broad reaches of the Pacific.

When it comes to assessing a storm's strength, the baseline that the World Meteorological Organization (WMO) has chosen for its record books is 925 millibars, a measurement that some modern scientific scales now refer to as hectopascals. Any storm eye whose pressure measures less than 925 millibars is one for the books, intense enough to be worthy of record. Using that measure alone, it's clear that the Pacific Ocean is host to the largest number of the world's truly intense tropical storms.

Since 1924, just twenty-three Atlantic Ocean hurricanes have qualified for the list of storms with eye pressures of less than 925 millibars. Only five of them—the Labor Day Hurricane of 1935 and hurricanes Allen, Gilbert, Rita, and

A dropsonde.

Wilma—were super-intense, with eye pressures of less than 900 millibars. The infamous pair of hurricanes Camille and Katrina, though they were hugely damaging and costly, did not figure in below the 900-millibar number. Hurricane Sandy did not even make the WMO cut, registering a comparatively benign 940 millibars in its nonspinning center.

The Portuguese explorer Ferdinand Magellan (1480-1521) led the first expedition to circumnavigate the world (although Magellan himself didn't make it all the way around, because he died along the way). In 1520, he sailed through straits near the tip of South America and entered an ocean unknown to him. The waters were calm at the time, so he called the body of water pacific, *which means peaceful. The Pacific Ocean, whose tropical storms are anything but peaceful, covers approximately 59 million square miles (95 million square kilometers).*

In the western north Pacific, however, atmospheric violence measured by intensely low eye pressure is much more common. Since 1950 there have been fifty-nine fully formed typhoons north of the equator. There have been twenty-five similarly rated cyclones in the western south Pacific and off

Australia since 1975. In the Atlantic, sub-925-millibar storms occur about once every five years. In the western Pacific, they are an annual event.

As the citizens of the Australian city of Darwin came to know only too well.

IN THE 1970s, Darwin was a tough little frontier town at the far Top End of Australia. Over the years it had suffered gamely through a variety of storms, natural and man-made. (During World War II, more Japanese bombs rained down on Darwin than on Pearl Harbor.) The weather in Darwin is perpetually hot and humid; the summertime rainy season that Darwinians still call "the wet" is frequently ripped apart by spectacular tropical thunderstorms. Cyclones are part of the usual pattern of midsummer weather—a midsummer that occurs in mid-December rather than July, since the city of Darwin is in the southern hemisphere.

When a gathering storm was first noticed out in the Arafura Sea off Darwin's northern seashore, at the start of a blisteringly hot Christmas week of 1974, no one thought it was anything special. The storm out in the sea was just a small one, and it was heading south, well away from the city. There would be rain in the western suburbs, perhaps, and fine displays of lightning. But that wasn't unusual; Darwin always had rain and lightning at this time of year. Each summer season had a full dozen cyclone alerts, and each time the Australian Broadcasting Corporation (ABC) sounded its sirens, the announcer went on air with the usual warnings about tying down loose objects and filling the bathtub with emergency water. Everyone heard but few listened. *The ABC was crying wolf,* people grumbled.

Fierce tropical cyclones regularly barreled in from the seas to the north and hammered the tin-roof shanties that were home to most of the forty-seven thousand Darwinians. Old-timers told of the unique sounds of a Darwin cyclone: the screeching of thousands of corrugated-iron roofs being gale-blown along the roadways; the noise of breaking glass; the endless howls of wind, of lashing rains; and, as endless background noise, the furious pounding of the ocean.

In 1974, as in years before, the locals were so familiar with bad weather, they generally took little notice of the radio.

The Australian Bureau of Meteorology tracked the storm as it passed slowly, still heading south. Most people remained complacent—it was Christmas, after all: there was church to attend, presents to wrap, trees to decorate, children to persuade to sleep.

But a few Darwinians suspected something was up.

The air in town felt somehow different. "Jerky" was how a nearby Chinese shopkeeper later described it. The songbirds fell strangely quiet. The Larrakia, the aboriginal people who like to camp in the tall grasses outside town, noticed that all the green ants they would normally have seen had vanished.

The clouds over Darwin were too high. They were strangely shaped and vivid with purples, greens, and other bizarre colors that just shouldn't have been there. Some people reported seeing what they described as a black velvet cloud hanging in the air about five miles (eight kilometers) above the sea. The dark cloud rolled, pulsed, and blotted out the sun.

Then, out at sea, the storm changed direction. Quite unexpectedly, it made a sharp right-angled swerve to the east and contracted: Cyclone Tracy then bore down with withering accuracy toward the dead center of Darwin.

The storm was the most dreadful and destructive event in all of Australian history. When the storm hit shore a little after midnight on what was now Christmas morning, it crushed building after building like a giant's hand smashing down from on high. Ten thousand houses, 80 percent of the city, were totally destroyed, reduced to matchsticks and pulverized concrete. The process was nearly identical, house after Christmas-decorated house: First, the roof was ripped off and whirled away into the rain-soaked night. Then the windows shattered, slicing people with slivers of glass. Next, the walls blew out. (People later described running in darkness and panic from room to room, locating the bathroom door by touch and racing inside, thinking that the smallest room would be the strongest—only to find that the outside wall was gone and they were facing a terrifying

Darwin, Australia, devastated by Cyclone Tracy.

frenzy of gales and fierce waves of hot pounding rain in the darkness beyond.)

Darwin was brought to its knees. Everything failed: The telephones were out. Electricity was down. Antennas were blown flat. Planes parked at the city airport were tossed about like toys, smashed beyond recognition. Ships broke loose in the harbor and either sank or drifted far from their moorings, useless. Many people who might have been helpful in the emergency were away for the Christmas holiday. The broadcast stations had only skeleton crews but no light or water; one station with a generator managed to get a message out to a remote sister station in the Australian outback. This tenuous link was the only communication Darwin had with the outside world for the first three days after the catastrophe.

When the first rescuers got there the day after the cyclone had hit, they saw that the physical destruction of Darwin was total. Seventy-one people had been killed. Roads were no more than pathways through miles of broken rubble and splintered timber. People wandered around, glassy-eyed, bewildered. Hundreds of dogs, frightened and unfed, emerged from the ruins to forage and menace the first rescuers with their snarling presence. There was a serious health threat of infection from typhoid and cholera. Police had to borrow guns from the nearby sheep ranches to deal with looters.

In the end, almost the entire city of Darwin had to be evacuated. Forty-one thousand of its forty-seven thousand inhabitants were without home, shelter, water, food, medicine, or communication. The Australian government arranged shuttles of aircraft—slowly at first, because the ruined Darwin airport could accommodate only one flight every ninety minutes. Over the next five days, a total of more than thirty-five thousand people were flown or driven out of the city—and by the time the year ended, Darwin had been all but emptied. More than half of those who left never came back.

Darwin, Australia, is a wholly rebuilt city now, slick and modern, where everything is claimed to be cyclone-proof—because, if nothing else, those who live at the Top End of Australia learned from the disaster of the 1970s that the Pacific can be a place of extraordinarily violent weather.

LARGE, SPRAWLING, ULTRA-LOW-PRESSURE storms like Cyclone Tracy occur five times more often in the Pacific than elsewhere in the world. They are also generally much more intense: thirty-seven of the northwest Pacific's fifty-nine modern-day typhoons have had pressures lower than 900 millibars.

Pacific storms have clearly been getting ever more menacing in recent years. Cyclone Tracy in 1974 was close to the beginning of this development: Typhoon Haiyan, which struck the Philippines in November 2013, suggests how truly ferocious things can get. The four decades between these two storms saw two developing trends: bigger and increasingly troublesome storms and an ever-greater accuracy in pinpointing where they might make landfall. More lives were at risk from the storms' gathering power; more lives were saved by the gathering boon of science.

Typhoon Tip, the deepest cyclonic storm of them all, recorded an eye-watering low pressure of just 870 millibars when it did its worst in waters off the Philippines in October 1979. With an edge-to-edge spread of 1,380 miles (2,220 kilometers), it enjoys the unique distinction of being both the deepest and the widest of all tropical storms on record. If Typhoon Tip were superimposed on a map of the United States, it would extend from the Mexican to the Canadian borders, and from Yosemite to the Mississippi River, its eye directly above Denver.

Typhoon Haiyan makes the point well. It was first spotted far away by observers in Hawaii. The four duty officers who arrived for their night shift in the early evening of Friday, November 1, 2013, in the drab Pearl Harbor building that houses the offices of the Joint Typhoon Warning Center were the first to notice something unusual. The satellite images for their routine sweep of the far western Pacific (where it was already the afternoon of the next day, Saturday) were just scrolling onto their monitors. Most of the ocean was quiet: just a single disorganized cluster of squalls, a small and nameless tropical storm, was wandering aimlessly westward toward the Philippine island of Mindanao. Then a new pattern of clouds appeared in the central ocean, and this one had an ominous look about it.

The proto-cyclone, if that is what this was, must have been developing rapidly during the day, for the earlier shift had reported nothing from the satellite when it had last transmitted pictures six hours previously. But now, quite clearly, wisps of cloud had arranged themselves in a way that suggested a definite and organized pattern was forming. The cloud formation was about 250 miles (400 kilometers) southeast of the tiny island of Pohnpei, in Micronesia, and it was changing its appearance fast. Real-time imagery then showed it assuming the all-too-familiar, vaguely swirling cyclonic appearance that betokens danger. The suddenness of this appearance and the fast lowering of pressure beneath the cover of clouds all struck the weather analysts as noteworthy, at the very least.

They promptly sent a message across the road to the operations room of the Pacific Fleet head-quarters: US Navy ships in the area might want to know that wind and rain could well affect any vessels heading for that area of the sea. A routine message. No alarms. Not yet.

By November 3, the Japan Meteorological Agency outside Tokyo had assigned the now-swirling wisps of cloud a number: Tropical Storm 31W. By the next day, the swirls had grown much more powerful, and the storm had been upgraded to full typhoon status. It was named Haiyan, the Chinese word for *petrel*, a seabird that in sailors' lore is

A satellite image of Typhoon Haiyan from November 8, 2013, with a map of the Philippines added.

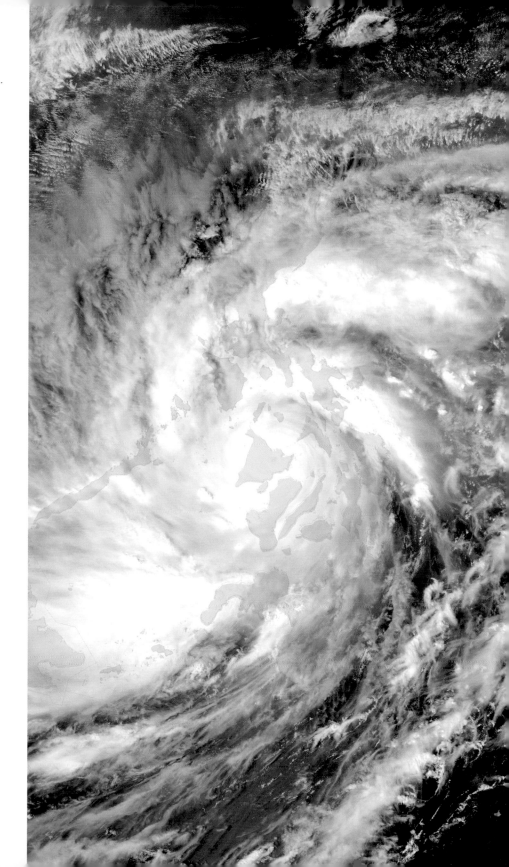

often associated with foul weather. Haiyan by now appeared to be moving in a westerly direction, traveling directly toward the barrier wall of the Philippine Islands. There, the local weather agency had confusingly decided to follow its own naming rules, not international rules. They called the storm Yolanda.

The situation was becoming alarming. The American and Japanese weather forecasters, and later those watching the big weather radars in China and Hong Kong, knew this was going to be a monster storm, no matter what it was called. They issued warnings to the civil defense agencies in the southern Philippines. The accuracy of their forecast meant crucial days of preparation for the onslaught of what was now clearly going to be a storm of a power seldom seen before at sea, and perhaps never before experienced on land.

Evacuations were ordered, and people began to stream away from the southeastern coasts of the Philippines, where the storm was predicted to land.

The forecasts were right, nearly to the minute. Typhoon Haiyan struck head on into the eastern Philippines, hitting the islands of Samar and Leyte almost simultaneously, at about nine a.m. on Friday, November 8, 2013. By the time it reached land, it had become the fiercest typhoon to have done so in the world's recorded history. When the northern eye wall of the storm struck the village of Guiuan, the anemometers (wind gauges) that hadn't blown off their bases and were still intact recorded wind gusts of 196 miles (315 kilometers) per hour—far greater than anything previously known.

Although the warnings and the precision of the forecasts

ABOVE LEFT AND RIGHT: Destruction in the wake of Typhoon Haiyan.

certainly helped keep down the total of human casualties, the physical and human damage was terrifying. Six and a half thousand people were killed, twenty-seven thousand were injured, and more than a thousand were missing. Just as in Darwin forty years before, whole cities were flattened, every building reduced to mere debris as if by an earthquake or an atom bomb. The city of Tacloban, the biggest in the region, was almost unrecognizable: first it was hit by the full force of the storm; then it was swamped by the corrosive seawaters of the thirteen-foot (four-meter) storm surge that followed.

Thanks once again to the accuracy of the forecasts, US Marines and US Navy ships were already on standby near mainland Japan and Okinawa, or they were out at sea. Once the signal came that the US State Department had agreed to respond to the Philippine government's official request for help, the well-oiled machinery of a full-blown American-led rescue operation was under way.

Operation Damayan, the twenty-one-million-dollar quick in-and-out rescue operation, formally began the next morning, Saturday, November 9. The night before, however, when a stunned Tacloban was still crawling out from under the storm's wreckage, a small flotilla of helicopters quietly brought in members of a US Special Forces team that was already in-country, secretly helping to deal with a long-running insurgency. Special Forces set up radios and began talking to the incoming armada of ships and the waves of marines and sailors. The relief operation involved twenty-two hundred US military personnel, thirteen warships, twenty-one helicopters, and the distribution of two thousand tons of American food, blankets, tents, generators, water purifiers, and other kinds of aid.

A US Marines Seahawk, part of Operation Damayan,
delivers supplies in Guiuan, Philippines.

The Pacific Ocean near American Samoa.

THERE IS A GROWING realization today that the world's weather is inextricably linked: weather *is* global. And the weather story of the planet begins in the world's biggest ocean, the Pacific.

The Pacific Ocean is broiled by the sun, whatever the season. Because the Earth tilts on its axis, the northern parts of the Pacific are broiled in the northern summer, the southern parts in the southern summer. The miles of ocean that lie between the Tropics of Cancer and Capricorn are broiled all the time.

The effect of the thermal energy that blasts endlessly down on Earth from the sun differs depending upon whether heat strikes solid or liquid below. When intense sunshine radiates down onto solid earth, the rocks become very hot, very quickly. Because of the physics of solids, they release this heat equally fast and return it to the atmosphere, retaining very little. To a wanderer in some hot deserts, a rock at nighttime can be blessedly cool. It's always different at sea.

When the same intense heat radiates down onto the ocean, the water warms slowly at first, but it retains the heat it absorbs for a long time. Because it is a moving liquid, it then shifts this captured heat around. The ocean's currents and its surface winds drive the captured thermal energy from side to side, either between the east and the west or the north and the south. Another, less well-known pattern of ocean movement known as thermohaline circulation can also shift this heat downward into the depths of the sea. Since the Pacific is by far the deepest ocean, as well as the broadest and longest, the amount of heat it can absorb and circulate within itself is almost beyond imagination.

Heat, in immeasurable quantities, is stored in the world's ocean generally, particularly in the Pacific, which occupies one-third of the planet's entire surface area. Much of this heat then warms the atmosphere. It does so especially where the ocean is subject to the most intense solar heating: that wide band of water between the tropics and along the equator, a band that shifts to the north and the south as the seasons change.

Within this well-defined area, the intense heat causes the seawater to evaporate and the warm air above it to rise. Immense clouds form and billow skyward. As they rise, air pressure lowers in the void the clouds leave behind. Cooler and heavier air then pours in from the north and the south to fill this low-pressure zone. Thanks to the west-to-east spinning of the Earth, this air tracks in a more or less westerly direction as it cascades inward: the air from the north heading toward the southwest, the air from the south tracking to the northwest. Since, as we've seen, winds are named for the direction they are coming from, these inrushings of cool air become the famous trade winds—the northeast trades in the northern hemisphere, the southeast trades below the equator.

This tropical-equatorial band is where the climatic business of the world begins. It is where the trade winds blow (or don't blow, if you hit the area of windless doldrums). It is where the monsoons begin their lives. It is where all the world's cyclones and hurricanes and typhoons are born. And in the Pacific portion of this area—by far the largest—a series of curious atmospheric and oceanic events occur that appear to be most crucial to the creation of the world's weather.

These occurrences are tangible, recognized, and recorded. As long ago as the late sixteenth century, South American fishermen working out of ports in the north of Peru, from Tumbes on the Ecuadorian border to Chimbote close to Lima, took note of what happened in the ocean waters. Their livelihoods depended on it—and modern weather science confirmed their findings.

Chimbote, Peru, came to be known as the world anchovy capital. The small silvery and smelly fish were found in staggering numbers in the cold waters just twenty miles (thirty-two kilometers) offshore; the little anchovies called anchovetas spawned a highly prosperous industry. Few fish have ever known such a boom: over the past century, Peruvian anchovy fisheries sprang up in every possible harbor along the coast. Thousands of fishermen worked the waters, eventually making the anchoveta the most exploited wild fish in the world. Thirteen million tons of the fish were hauled into the nets in 1971; most of it was ground into fish meal, or sent off to fertilize fields or feed livestock all across the world.

But the abundance of anchovies was a fitful thing. Chimbote fishermen saw that once every five or six years, usually in November or December, the anchovetas vanished. One day, there would be darts of quicksilver shoals all around; the next, nothing but the blue silence of the deep. And there was another thing: at the same time, the cold waters offshore that brought in the evening fog became warmer. The fogs vanished, the skies cleared.

The lack of catch frustrated the fishermen, to be sure, and they cursed their empty nets. But the absence of anchovetas had an effect that then spread all the way up the food chain.

Hauling in anchovies in Chimbote, Peru.

The gannets, cormorants, and pelicans that fed on the anchovies died, or they abandoned their nests. Chicks died waiting as their parents made futile long-distance searches for food. Squid, turtles, and even small sea mammals died also, because the water was too warm for them or there wasn't enough food. These dead creatures floated to the surface in large numbers, creating small islands of decay, their gases so acidic, they blistered the paint on boat hulls. To the fishermen, the loss of anchovies was an economic disaster; but the smorgasbord of other deaths and absences—together with the disfigurement of their boats—made the event seem both curious and sinister. Because this phenomenon invariably arrived around the celebration of Christ's birth, the fishermen, with a touch of bitter humor, called it *El Niño de Navidad*, "the Christmas Child."

"El Niño" to describe the change in the weather was a phrase that first made it into the English language at the end of the nineteenth century, not so much for the fishermen's misery but because of the specific reason for it: the change of the current in the waters below.

The cold waters of the Humboldt Current, part of the normal pattern of Pacific circulation, powerfully sweep Antarctic waters northward along the South American coast before heading west along the equator. During El Niño, this oceanic movement would be mysteriously disrupted. Instead the Humboldt Current would be replaced, or nudged farther out to sea, by an irruption of warm water. This warm water bullied its way down from the equator and smothered the upwelling of cold-water nutrients on which the anchovies fed. The little fish then went elsewhere, well beyond the reach of the Peruvian fishing boats.

At first it was simply this change of current and unusual warming of the ocean that was called El Niño. Then in the mid-twentieth century, oceanographers and climatologists realized that the change of currents off Peru was just one of many features of a much larger and more important phenomenon.

Many names are associated with the research that confirmed this. One person in particular is Gilbert Walker, a mathematician; a designer of flutes; a keen student of the boomerang and of the flight paths of ancient Celtic spears; an authority on the aerodynamics of birds' wings and the formation of clouds; an advocate of both the sports of skating and gliding, and the use of statistics; and a civil servant in British India. Walker had a meteorological epiphany in 1924 that helped secure what would become the Pacific Ocean's reputation as weather generator for the world.

Walker was appointed Director General of Observatories, India, in 1904, and spent twenty years puzzling over a mathematical means of predicting the monsoon. (He was inspired to do so because after the monsoon failed to arrive in 1900, a terrible famine had followed as a result.) While he did not solve the mysteries of the monsoon, Walker's work still led to a globally significant discovery.

Based on his exhaustive analysis of decades of weather records from all across the British Empire, Walker was able to show that El Niño events that occurred off the Peruvian coast—the fishermen's accounts were by now well known to scientists around the world were in fact part of an enormous and all-encompassing transpacific set of weather patterns. These patterns turned out to be like a marine mirror. If something meteorological was happening on one side of the ocean, the exact opposite was happening on the other side. The same held true meteorologically across seasons or extended periods.

Periods of ocean warming here led to cooling ocean there. The Peruvian sea starvation during a locally warm-sea El

Niño event would in time be followed by a local sea cooling and return to abundance, and that would be called (keeping to the Christmas-themed naming practice) La Niña. Floods on one side of the ocean led to droughts on the other. There were periodic swings in weather and in the human response to it. Sometimes there were more cyclones; sometimes there were fewer. There were years of failed monsoons and years of summertime drenching; periods of famine and periods of abundance; dust bowl summers, harvest-rich autumns, prosperity and ruin, peace and turmoil. Within the Pacific, around the Pacific's coasts, and even, perhaps, beyond them and around the globe.

Sir Gilbert Thomas "Boomerang" Walker declared in the early 1920s that this was due to a previously unrecognized natural phenomenon. What drove the regular and dramatic changes in the Pacific weather, Walker said, must be some kind of repeating mechanism up in the atmosphere. Whatever it was, this pattern of invisible winds and movements seemed to operate as a kind of seesaw, a beam-engine balance moving around a central pivot that lay somewhere in the center of the ocean.

This axis seemed to hover around where the International Date Line crosses the equator, in the middle of that sprawl of limestone specks then known as the Gilbert Islands and the Phoenix Islands, now the Republic of Kiribati. Up on this side meant down on the other; high pressure here meant low pressure there; hot here, cool across the other side; cruelly wet in this place, bone-dry in that. It had a beautiful logic to it, and measurements taken over the years that followed have long proved Walker right.

The transpacific atmospheric wind pattern Walker discovered was eventually named the Walker Circulation in his honor. This wind pattern produced the back-and-forth,

The Walker Circulation

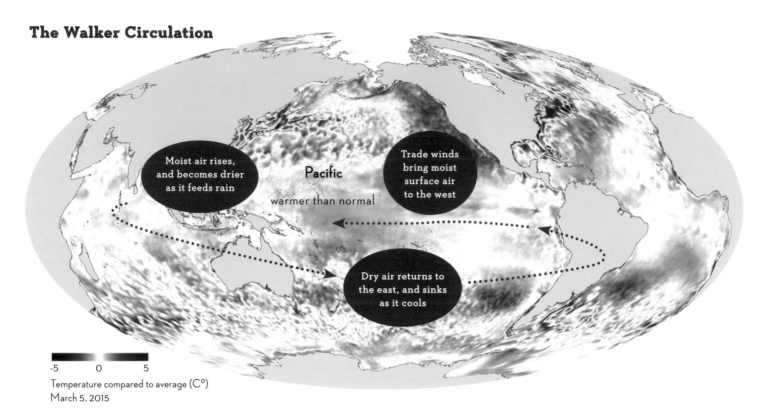

Moist air rises, and becomes drier as it feeds rain

Trade winds bring moist surface air to the west

Pacific

warmer than normal

Dry air returns to the east, and sinks as it cools

-5   0   5

Temperature compared to average (C°)
March 5, 2015

hot-and-cold, wet-and-dry, stormy-and-serene periods that seemed to dominate the tropical Pacific's weather, which Walker named the Southern Oscillation.

The initials of Southern Oscillation combined with the initials of El Niño form ENSO, the acronym for what is undeniably Earth's most important climatic phenomenon. If the Pacific is the generator of the world's weather, then ENSO represents the turbines that power the generator, and the Walker Circulation is the force that sets the turbines spinning in the first place.

The Walker Circulation is caused by the existence of long-lasting cells of pressure in certain places around the ocean. There is generally high atmospheric pressure over the eastern Pacific. There is generally a large low-pressure area over the western Pacific, most notably around the sea-

spattered islands of Indonesia and the Philippines, the area that oceanographers and meteorologists like to call the Maritime Continent. The air above the ocean then moves, as physics demands, from the high-pressure area to the low, in other words from east to west. The trade winds at the surface, which blow nearly constantly in this direction, are this movement's very visible and familiar manifestation.

As the trade winds blow, they help push the warm waters of the tropical seas below them in the same direction. Incredible though this may sound, the sea then piles up very slowly and deliberately as a huge wave of water passes steadily across and into the western edges of the ocean. The western Pacific can sometimes be a full two feet higher than the waters in the east. Some of this warm water evaporates and helps create the giant cyclonic storms and typhoons, like

El Niño caused deadly flooding and mudslides in northern California (March 1998).

Tracy and Haiyan, that form over the western seas. Some of the warm water dives down into the ocean, cools, and is returned to the east via deep ocean currents. In a normal series of years, this pattern is repeated again and again: the Walker Circulation of the air above; the migration of the seawater below; the explosive growth of storms in the far west Pacific; and the return of the cool and dry air and upwelling cool water (and the anchovies!) to the Pacific east. Calm and stability of a kind reigns.

But for unexplained reasons, the Walker Circulation sometimes changes. The trade winds weaken or falter or even reverse their directions, and then an El Niño period occurs, and the system changes with it . . . dramatically. Or the Walker Circulation can sometimes strengthen in the opposite manner and with equal drama; then the reverse, the phenomenon of La Niña, dominates the weather picture instead.

Tracking, measuring, and predicting the arrival of El Niño and La Niña has lately become a major element in worldwide weather forecasting and climate modeling. It is safe and reasonable to say that in the computation of the planet's weather, all eyes are all the time on what is happening in the Pacific and on the behavior of the Southern Oscillations. A major El Niño event is said to be starting at around the time this book is being written (late summer 2015), and around the planet, concerned people are watching anxiously. For as the Pacific oscillates, so oscillates the world.

AMERICA'S
NATIONAL STORM

I used to live in Tulsa, Oklahoma, in the 1960s, when we knew much less about tornadoes than we do now. I remember a group of us standing out in the yard as the oily-looking clouds growled their way overhead and we watched for the tendrils beginning to snake their way downward. "There's one—look!" someone would cry. And there would be the menacing down-tube twirling and flailing in the air. It would falter, still itself, and turn back up to be re-absorbed into the upper storms. I always thought it looked like a teacher's wagging finger in the sky, telling us to watch out below.

Hurricanes and typhoons are always born in the ocean and they can be massive, and when they make landfall, they do terrible damage over vast areas. Tornadoes are always born on land, and are generally very small dangling tubes of high-speed horror lowering from inside thunderclouds. Their tiny concentrations of deadliness can do astonishing amounts of damage in small, tightly focused areas of human settlement.

Hurricanes and typhoons wreak their terrors around the planet, but most of the world's tornadoes occur in the United States. If anyone held so gruesome a contest, there would be a clear winner: the tornado is America's national storm.

Tornadoes can occur almost anywhere in the lower forty-eight states. A tornado that touched down in Natchez, Mississippi, in 1840 killed 317 people, although it was actually even more deadly, since this is only the number of white people who died. The twister is known to have killed many slaves, but statistics back in those unenlightened times did not include their deaths. The infamous Tri-State Tornado of March 1925 killed 695 people and injured more than 2,000

A violent tornado hit northeast South Dakota on June 23, 2002.

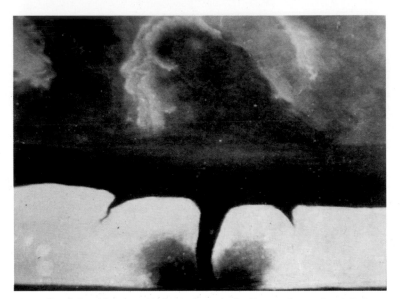

Considered the oldest known photo of a tornado. It was taken in South Dakota on August 28, 1884. The origins of the word tornado are a little confusing; it comes from the Spanish words either for "thunder" or for "turning." Both are applicable, since tornadoes really are the fast-turning spawn of thunderstorms.

as it swept across Missouri, Illinois, and Indiana. As of this writing, five other tornadoes have killed more people. There are even scars in the forests near where I live in western Massachusetts, still visible fifteen years after we were hit by a lethal but, in our neck of the woods, very rare tornado.

But these storms tend to cluster, usually in the hot summertime, in just eight states: Texas, Kansas, Oklahoma, Iowa, Missouri, South Dakota, Colorado, and Nebraska. Geography has turned this area into Tornado Alley, where inhabitants live in the perpetual path of these extraordinary storms.

Take Joplin, Missouri, as an example. Joplin is a city nearly in the middle of the nation, the midpoint of a triangle formed by Kansas City, Missouri; Little Rock, Arkansas; and Oklahoma City, Oklahoma. It had been an Ozark Moun-

tains boomtown, briefly the lead and zinc mining capital of the world, and once home to the gangsters Bonnie and Clyde. By 2010, around fifty thousand Midwesterners were living there.

May 22, 2011, in Joplin was a rainy day from hell. It was warm and muggy. Enormous dark clouds swept in from the west. The air was full of foreboding—all the familiar signs that a storm could develop.

Government monitors at the National Weather Service Storm Prediction Center (NWS SPC) in Norman, Oklahoma, were watching closely. They had already placed the counties around Joplin under an official tornado watch. Everyone on the ground knew what the NWS SPC scientists knew: that the lowering clouds over the city were likely filled with what have come to be known as supercells. These enormous rotating thunderstorms, with torrential rains at the edges and sweeping squall lines all folded inside ominous-looking thick black billowing curtains, hide the terrible dangers of tornado formation.

Most people in Joplin got on with their daily routines; they were used to this kind of thing, after all. But they kept their eyes open for any signs of telltale funnels forming in the turbulent gray underside of the huge clouds. Everyone had the NOAA radio on. If the alarm signal sounded, if the tornado watch was changed to a tornado warning, if there were credible reports that a funnel cloud had been spotted, it was time to take action. Go down to the storm shelter that many people had in their basements. Stay there while the crashing and thrashing of the wind did its worst above. Hope to surface once the storm had passed, and assess the damage. Stay alive.

As the afternoon wore on, the storm chasers in and around Joplin started their engines. These curious and fool-

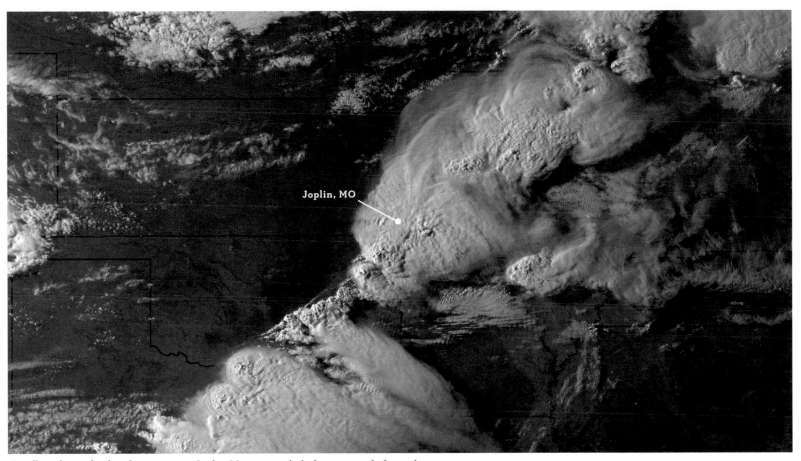

Satellite photo of a thunderstorm over Joplin, Missouri, right before a tornado formed.

hardy teams in their big armored SUVs liked to identify, follow, and film the most savage twisters. Their motives were mixed: some were merely curious daredevils; others perhaps hoped to help, to be the frontliners for the more cautious observers at the NWS; still other storm chasers hoped to get that fabulous newsworthy shot, the enduring image of catastrophe that would bring in a substantial check from the local TV station.

For a while the weather seemed to toy with its potential victims. Every so often a funnel-shaped depression in the cloud base appeared and headed toward the ground. But each time, the "finger" withdrew up into its sleeve of cloud.

But at 5:14 p.m., the civil defense sirens began to wail in Joplin: the long initial blast, then the rising-and-falling, rising-and-falling sound. There was now no doubt. The fingers of doom were coming too close to the ground. One, maybe more, would touch down and gain hold, like the suction tube the storm actually was, and begin a lethal passage across town.

HURRICANES ARE BEST measured by the pressure at their center or by their wind speed. But tornadoes nowadays are informally rated by the damage they cause. Tornado winds are much, much higher than hurricane winds and have proved nearly impossible to measure. Even the sturdiest of anemometers, or wind-speed instruments, is invariably destroyed by the strongest tornado.

The Enhanced Fujita (EF) Scale, which rates storms according to their wind-generated damage, has been used in the United States since 2007.

There has never been a tornado stronger than an EF5.

(EF0) (65-85 mph)

(EF1) Moderate tornado (86-110 mph)

(EF2) Significant tornado (111-135 mph)

(EF3) Severe tornado (136-165 mph)

(EF4) Devastating tornado (166-200 mph)

(EF5) Incredible tornado (201+ mph)

Tornado near Friona, Texas (August 2009).

Houses in Joplin, Missouri, leveled by the tornado.

Twenty minutes later, that happened. A long gray-and-orange tube reached down, connected with the ground near a country club in the southwest part of town, and began to churn across the city, gathering size and power as it roared its terrifying way eastward.

And then, in the fading light of that midsummer evening in Joplin, Missouri, matters very quickly got much, much worse.

The tornado funnel suddenly started to widen. Some of the storm chasers reported seeing two or three separate vortices within its ragged and fast-growing lower end. The swirling that blew tree branches around and threw them up into the air became much more complex. Branches were hurled in all directions as more and more spirals formed within the main funnel. As the spirals multiplied, the growing beast whirled faster and faster and faster. The EF scale numbers climbed.

Real, serious, memorable, dreadful damage was happening.

The winds snapped power poles, and trees—whole trees, not just branches—broke. The lights went out. Televisions and radios were silenced. The noise outside grew louder and louder. People later compared it to an out-of-control express train hurtling through the city, roaring and crashing ceaselessly. Roofs were torn off, trailer homes were flipped and upended, and before long, whole houses were being ripped apart, their walls flattened, their chimneys torn down and thrown to the ground.

After chewing up hundreds of houses, the fast-moving storm grew even stronger and attacked solid brick-built commercial structures: windows blew out, and walls bent and buckled and were then torn away; then whole structures collapsed, their contents hurled up to vanish into the gray coiling skies. Steel supports were bent and folded like tissue paper, thick reinforcing bars twisted like the rolled-up lids of sardine cans. A parked semitrailer was picked up and flown into the sky, where it whirled and twisted. The falling truck was then slammed into a tree from which all the bark had been stripped; it folded completely around the trunk, like gum around a pencil.

Feats of strength that normally required gigantic industrial machines proved child's play for the storm. The heavy concrete stops in parking lots, each of them bolted into the pavement, were wrenched from the ground and tossed into the air like confetti. Manhole covers were sucked up into space, thrown not hundreds of yards but actual miles away. Edges of cardboard boxes and chair legs were found deeply embedded in stucco walls. Cars were casually tossed. School

An aerial photograph shows the tornado's path of destruction.

President Barack Obama meets with residents dealing with the destruction caused by the massive tornado that passed through Joplin, Missouri, on May 22, 2011, killing at least 160 people.

buses and tractor trailers were sent spinning into the air. Churches, warehouses, strip malls, a school, hospital buildings, a Walmart, a Home Depot, cell phone towers, apartment complexes—almost everything in the tornado's path was wrecked beyond recognition.

And people died: 160 according to the city. Another 1,150 were injured. Eighty people died in their homes as the buildings collapsed around them. Six hospital patients on ventilators suffocated when the power went out and the backup generators failed. Students from a graduation ceremony held nearby who had sought shelter from the ominous-looking clouds were trapped at a school. Some of those who lived had inspiring stories to tell: the accounts of the young teachers who covered whimpering and terrified children with their own bodies as debris flew and battered them and gale-force blasts tore at them for what seemed like endless hours served as a powerful reminder of human heroism.

The tornado finally lifted and drew back up into the

clouds at 6:12 p.m. It had covered twenty-two miles (thirty-five kilometers) in thirty-eight terrible minutes, leaving behind a straight line of destruction from west to east. The trail of damage and death was just a few hundred yards south of the heart of the city. It leveled not just the major business centers but more cruelly the parts of Joplin where people lived and shopped and worshipped and went to school. A total of 6,954 houses were destroyed, nearly 900 others damaged. One-quarter of the city was fully razed to the ground; the total cost was reckoned at 2.8 billion dollars, the costliest tornado in recorded history.

How strong was the Joplin tornado of 2011, and how fast were its wind speeds? Debates about this went on for months as meteorologists assessed the damage to the tiniest extent. How much force would it take to rip a hundred-pound manhole from its moorings, or to send a parking stop slab careening for a mile through the air? How fast does the wind need to be to lift an eighteen-wheeler and wrap it completely around a tree trunk? How much force will reduce an entire house to little more than finely chopped firewood?

The conclusion was that the Joplin tornado had indeed been of the very worst, very strongest, and rarest variety, an EF5 on the damage-index scale. To achieve the level of damage experienced in this wrecked little city would have required winds to be at the very least 200 miles (320 kilometers) per hour, maybe even as high as 250 miles (400 kilometers) per hour. Unimaginable compared to hurricanes, which seldom muster gales of even half that speed.

WHY IS IT America that is so affected? Tornadoes do occur elsewhere, as do their maritime counterparts, the waterspouts. The deadliest tornado in recorded world history happened in Bangladesh in April 1989, when 1,300 people were killed; nearly 13,000 were injured; 80,000 were left homeless; and vast tracts of muddy farmland were shaved as if by a giant razor, with every standing thing, house, tree, warehouse, and mosque flattened. This impoverished country between India and Burma is at the upper end of the funnel-shaped portion of the Bay of Bengal. It has experienced more than its fair share of tornado-related damage: five of the world's ten biggest tornadoes occurred there, and almost four thousand people have died as a direct result of their malign visitations.

Fourteen of the world's fifty worst tornadoes have occurred in America, however. When you consider all the twisters that have ever been recorded—including the relatively modestly powered versions, the EF0s and EF1s—then there is no doubt: though Bangladesh and Russia and China and Brazil suffer the effects of these extraordinary storms, the American Midwest is hit by the most tornadoes. More than twelve hundred of these strange stormlike events occur in the middle of the United States each year.

Why? The reason is quite simply because of an accident of geography. No place else on Earth is topographically and climatically arranged quite the same as the United States. The country has long barriers of mountain chains enclosing the immense and unobstructed Mississippi River Valley. It is poised between the tropical south and the subarctic north, which allows air collisions and wind generation that occur almost nowhere else with such regularity and certainty.

Cold air from the Canadian prairies intersects with moisture-laden warm air from the Gulf of Mexico. These two combining wind masses are steered westward by the prevailing breezes from across the Rocky Mountains. Huge rain-heavy cumulonimbus clouds form, and the Coriolis effect starts them spinning. Thunderstorms and squalls

A topographic map of the United States.

develop. Uninhibited by any sudden elevation changes in the Mississippi River Valley below, the long fingers of brown-gray rain clouds spin themselves as they are born from the rotating storm above, and spiral down to earth. Tornado Alley is where they march each summer, and the damage they wreak there has become part of the American legend, part of the American story. It always was, and it always will be.

Knowledge of tornadoes goes back a long way in North America. And though we modern folk depend on forecasts and high technology and satellites, there was an earlier body of knowledge among American Indians that should not be entirely discounted. The plains-dwelling Kiowa, for instance, had a name for tornadoes, the *Mánkayía*, and regarded the storms as the powerful work of a great horse spirit, a great medicine horse. In the late nineteenth century, a Kiowa war party returning from a raid told a visiting American anthropologist, James Mooney, of suddenly "hearing a roar that sounded like a buffalo in the rutting season. Sloping down from the cloud a

Kiowa great horse spirit.

sleeve appeared, its center red; from this[,] lightning shot out. The tremendous funnel tore through the timber bordering the Washita [River], heaving trees into the air."

Generally speaking, nomadic American Indians, well aware of the frequency of tornado touchdowns, left what we now call Tornado Alley during the summertime, and made their way to the north of the Dakotas and northern Minnesota, where the climate is more stable during the summer. But others, like the Cheyenne, who have a long tradition of talking to storms, and the Kiowa, dealt with the inrushing catastrophes more directly, more robustly.

"Some of the men wanted to run away," James Mooney was told. "But the older, more experienced Kiowas knew what must be done. They called for everybody to try hard and brace themselves. The elders drew their pipes from saddlebags and lit them. They raised their pipes to the storm spirit, entreating it to smoke, and to go around them. The cloud heard their prayers . . . and passed by."

The Wichita stage a ceremony in which an elder will hurl an ax into the ground, splitting the storm in two. The Apache and Comanche have secret rituals that interest the scientists at the NWS SPC in Oklahoma. Discussions have taken place in recent years between forecasters and tribal elders who claim a disproportionate degree of success in persuading, as they see it, storms to bypass their communities and spare those who are respectful of their power.

And if science doesn't quite buy into the idea that persuasion is the key, there is no disrespect intended. Far better to run and hide, the meteorologists say, to get out of the way of these incredibly powerful works of nature. Far better still, say many of the Indian elders, never to have settled here at all. For there are places in the world so dangerous and so frequently subject to the wrath of the breaking skies and shaking earth, they might as well remain pristine, meant for the buffalo and the bald eagle alone. Places where we can display our respect to the power of the planet by keeping well away.

OUT ON THE
FAR HORIZON

Back in the 1930s an Oxford geology professor on an expedition to the high Arctic discovered an unusual outcrop of rock in East Greenland. The Skaergaard Intrusion, as it was named, was thought to be full of precious metals like gold and palladium, making it worth millions. Had it not been covered, that is, in hundreds of feet of snow and ice.

Eighty years passed. The planet and the oceans have become much warmer. Glaciers have shrunk. Corals are dying. Bird populations are changing. The polar ice cap has broken up. Ships are now able to navigate the once-impassible Northwest Passage between the Atlantic and the Pacific.

And the Skaergaard Intrusion is now free of ice and snow.

In 2011 an Australian company won an exploitation contract from the Greenland government and set up a small mining camp. A group of a dozen Australians began drill-ing experimental holes into the Skaergaard rocks. One late evening a sudden unexpected sound woke the sleeping men in the camp. It was the sound of many sharp claws scrap-ing the exposed rock surface. A huge number of angry polar bears had appeared out of nowhere and were advancing on the camp, clearly insisting that these human invaders get out.

The men did get out in time (though mining efforts have since resumed), but the bear invasion was a reminder of a new world reality: that global warming is a phenomenon that produces many often unimagined consequences. The state of the world's weather is currently very much one of them.

The combination of warming and sea-level rise and a troubling increase in the acidity of the oceanic waters—caused by the sea absorbing some of the carbon dioxide pumped out by industry—is having an enormous impact around the world. Countries are drowning: the island

An iceberg in Greenland.

Admiral Samuel Locklear (left) with Defense Secretary Chuck Hagel in Honolulu, Hawaii, in September 2013.

Republic of Kiribati in the Central Pacific, for instance, will have to be evacuated before most of the readers of this book retire. Bangladesh is shrinking because the rising waters of the Bay of Bengal are submerging entire tracts of coastal jungle. The warming is breaking up the ice fields in Antarctica, shrinking the coverage of the peaks of Greenland, melting the world's glaciers, and changing landscapes that had been stable for centuries. And it is alarming senior admirals in the American military.

In early 2013, Samuel Locklear III, the American four-star admiral who was at the time in charge of all US forces in and around the Pacific (that's nearly four hundred thousand Navy, Army, Marine, and Air Force personnel ranged around more than half the world), spoke to security specialists and analysts at Harvard and Tufts Universities. Locklear said he and his fellow officers had recently detected a new pattern in the number and scale of Pacific typhoons: "We are already on super typhoon twenty-seven or twenty-eight here in the Western Pacific. The average is about seventeen. Weather patterns are more severe than they have been in the past."

Studying the impact of climate change in the Arctic.

Admiral Locklear went on to make what many people at the time thought was a highly eccentric prediction. In spite of all the political tensions between China and Japan, between North and South Korea, between Beijing and Washington, in the admiral's considered view, it was changes to the climate, changes that were suggested by these typhoon clusters, that posed the greatest of all security threats in the region.

Significant upheaval related to the warming planet, the admiral intimated, "is probably the thing most likely to happen . . . and that will cripple the security environment. Probably that will be more likely than the other scenarios we all often talk about." A ripple of amazement coursed through Washington. Significantly, no one in the White House or the Pentagon, however, chose to challenge the admiral's view.

The subject of the world's weather—or, more properly, the world's climate, of which weather is a day-to-day feature—has become ever more urgent. We know for a fact that the world is warming. Its temperature has risen, in fits and starts, by nine-tenths of a degree since the early years of the last century. During more recent years the sea level has also started to rise. Polar ice caps, melting under the influence of the planet's warming, pump more water into the ocean each year, bringing sea levels up by about a foot every decade. And the seawater itself, affected by human-produced gases in the atmosphere, is becoming ever more acidic.

Rising sea levels will change regional and global politics. Where will people go after their country is submerged? How do countries deal with their ever-

Sea ice in the Greenland Sea. The ten years between 2005 and 2015 included nine of the lowest summer seasonal ice coverings on record.

changing shapes? Who will be fighting over an ocean basin's ever-deepening offshore oil fields? How will our ships operate if storms get worse and worse? How will countries affected by foul weather deal with the poverty and dislocation if the storms that hit them get ever fiercer?

The connection between global warming and the frequency and ferocity of storms is a major focus of climate research these days. Lately, to handle the incredibly complex mathematics needed to calculate the details of this connection, a number of very impressive computers have been put to work. One of the more magnificent of these is located just to the west of Tokyo, at the Japan Agency for Marine-Earth Science and Technology (JAMSTEC).

The JAMSTEC computer is called the Earth Simulator 2 (ES2). This remarkable and entirely Japanese-made machine, which keeps being improved and upgraded, currently can calculate at the truly fantastic speed of 131 tFLOPS. A tFLOP, short for teraFLOP, is the measure used to describe a supercomputer's power. A tFLOP donotes the machine's ability to perform one trillion Floating-point Operations Per Second. (A floating-point operation is one that involves a number with a decimal point in it, and so is more complicated: 2 times 3 is easy; 2.3 times 3.4, a floating-point operation, is more complex.) A recent live test showed that the ES2 can output global weather analyses of incredibly complex detail. Several times a day the supercomputer produces a three-dimensional map of the world's atmosphere, showing the climatic details every three miles (five kilometers) horizontally and through more than one hundred slices of the atmosphere vertically.

The ES2 is so costly a creation, and Japan is so seismically unstable an island chain, that its guardians protect it as if it were the *Mona Lisa* or the Hope Diamond. The computer sits inside its own building, which is on gimbals and rubber legs to keep it level in the event of an earthquake or typhoon. The building has metal-mesh ceiling nets to diffuse lightning strikes, and special metal shields to keep stray magnetic fields at bay.

Thus swaddled, Japan's ES2 quietly crunches away at the streams of data from the world's weather watcher. Its operators continue to try to divine, as do many others in similar laboratories around the world, whether the onset of El Niño or La Niña cannot merely be declared to be under way but shown to be about to happen. Can it be predicted, in other words, just like any other weather forecast? No one yet has come up with a way to forecast the onset of ENSO. At a time when the worldwide weather has become such a worldwide obsession, this is a major concern. For when El Niño arrives, it wreaks havoc—everywhere.

Most recently the Japanese team working on El Niño has been able to show that the onset of an ENSO warm phase is often preceded by a machine-gun-like series of small and intense storms north of Australia, in the waters off Papua New Guinea. The storms are small enough to be known as westerly wind bursts (WWB). For a while they were dismissed as random events, unconnected to the happenings on the far side of the ocean; but nowadays they are thought to be linked to—or, at least, to coincide with—much larger meteorological events. Whether these little WWBs actually indicate the onset of El Niño, or whether they are the result of the onset of El Niño, is a matter of much debate within the meteorological community.

El Niño effects have been noticed for centuries. A supposed El Niño in 1877 triggered a two-year drought in China and the starvation deaths of nine million people. The pattern of the phenomenon bears repeating: the inflow of warm water in the eastern Pacific halts the cold upwelling rush of nutrients, and all the anchovetas vanish from the waters off Peru; other sea

NOAA buoys measure ocean temperatures at various depths to help predict onsets of El Niño or La Niña.

creatures die, the noxious gases from their rotting carrion bubble up from the sea, and boats have their paint blistered by the scum of the acidity.

Globally, a host of other phenomena can also develop, probably linked to El Niño–related changes in the Pacific Ocean, the world's biggest expanse of seawater. And an expanse, it is worth mentioning again, of heat-catching seawater—and trapping solar heat is ultimately what this meteorological drama is all about.

During El Niño, there can be, among other things, major flooding on the South American west coast when the current-warmed humid breezes rise above the Andes Mountains, where the humidity then condenses and falls as rain or snow. During the onset phase, there can be droughts in northern Brazil, but severe rainstorms near Rio de Janeiro in southern coastal Brazil. Cyclones and typhoons tend to form in the Pacific more centrally than usual during an ENSO warm phase, and since the storms spend a longer time tracking their way westward over larger expanses of warmer seas, they can grow, accelerate, and deepen more—and be much more violent and destructive when finally they reach land.

The 1982–83 El Niño, one of the strongest ever known, was memorable for its cascade of events. The trade winds weakened. Sea levels in the eastern Pacific began to rise, up to a foot higher along the coast of Ecuador. Eastern sea temperatures shot up. Off the coast of Peru, fur seals and sea lions began to die. Deserts in eastern South America were drenched with rain. Grasshoppers swarmed. Toad population numbers went through the roof. Mosquitoes came in clouds; malaria cases skyrocketed.

There were droughts and forest fires in Java. Terrible storms wrecked the coastline of California; there was flooding in the American Deep South; and ski resorts in the northeast United States reported warmer weather and lackluster business. All told, the economic costs of the 1982–83 El Niño were estimated by the US government at eight billion dollars. And, of course, for every malaria death in Ecuador or village burning in Sulawesi, the cost was boundless misery.

Even during relatively modest El Niño events, the effects can be widespread and unexpected. Drought can affect Hawaii, drastically lowering the sugar harvest. Forest fires can and do sweep across Borneo in Southeast Asia; monsoon-dependent crops can wither and fail in India. Sea lions and elephant seals die off in the waters off California, and unanticipated fish and squid appear in the waters off Oregon and British Columbia.

The polar jet stream can be nudged farther southward during an El Niño event, making winters in Canada more acutely cold and forcing more rain to fall in the southern states, cooling everything down, including shortening the growing season for Florida oranges. At the same time, North-

El Niño of 2009-10 caused severe winter erosion along the California coastline.

ern Europe is colder and drier; and in Africa, Kenya is wetter, Botswana drier. The lists of El Niño effects are endless and at times, seemingly contradictory. The concern is global.

As is the concern about global warming. Most mathematical models say that by the end of this century, the central

NOAA and the French space agency Centre National d'Études Spatiales launched the Jason-3 satellite on January 17, 2016, to continue a multi-decade satellite study of sea-level rise and other climate-change factors.

tropical Pacific will have risen in temperature by as much as 5.4 degrees Fahrenheit (3 degrees Celsius). The level of the sea will have risen between one and three feet. How will those two long-term changes affect or be affected by El Niños that can be expected during the remaining decades of the century? Much of the world's weather is born of this phenomenon. So it would be extremely valuable to know about all and any of the substantial changes like these—especially if they are changes that are either caused by El Niño, or that are even the ultimate cause of it.

The Earth Simulator 2 and other computers and machines around the world hum ceaselessly, trying to find the answers to these essential questions. One observation that has produced consistent enough results to be called a discov-

ery is that the Walker Circulation has steadily weakened over the last sixty years. It has done so—with weakening trade winds the most obvious demonstration of this—at a rate entirely consistent with the rising temperature of the surface of the Pacific. A weaker Walker Circulation is linked with the start of an El Niño. This suggests, to put it most bluntly, that the world could find itself in a state of more or less permanent El Niño conditions if the trend persists. That, with its history of more extreme weather in the western Pacific and over the North American continent—to say nothing of a total collapse of the Peruvian fish meal industry—could cause long-term changes to human behavior, from where we build our cities to when and where we plant our crops.

But little is certain. Thanks to the computers, and to the

fascination with Pacific weather, global forecasting is less of an enigma, less of a throw of the dice, than it once was. But out in the Pacific, it still remains a mystery of daunting complexity.

However, among a growing number of climatologists, there is an agreement these days about heat, the radiation from the sun, and the manner in which the planet deals with it. Many scientists who study climate and weather now believe that because of its immense appetite for absorbing heat, the Pacific Ocean could end up as the savior of the world's living creatures. It will do so by taking in all that destructive heat from the sun and from the excesses of our carbon emissions. Rather than allowing the heat to scorch dead the inhabited Earth, the ocean will employ it to slowly warm itself up. The Pacific will carry the world's heat burden on its own.

The short-term effects of all this local absorption of heat will be dramatic, though. There will be bigger and more destructive typhoons, with super-Tracys, with stupendous Haiyans. There will perhaps be a more urgent need for evacuations of islands that will be inundated more swiftly than predicted. Maybe there will be bigger snowfalls in the Cascade and the Sierra mountain ranges in the western United States. Maybe no anchovies will ever be caught again off Peru. Maybe the forests of Sarawak will be consumed by fire.

For now, it is cities around the Atlantic Ocean that seem to be taking the threat of weather-related mayhem most seriously. There are currently some forty climate-change-related construction schemes under way in ocean-side cities around the world. Amsterdam in the Netherlands is one of the cities doing the most: building shopping malls that float, creating parks designed to absorb floodwaters, making diversion dams and canals to sluice away excess rainwater. Central to all these preparations—whether they are advanced, whether they incorporate revolutionary designs, whether they are likely to work—is the assumption that the worst will happen to each city when the weather gets bad. The climate experts in all these coastal cities loudly assert that the weather is *already* getting bad. As the world warms, as the ice melts, and as the sea levels rise, complicated physical changes are happening. We may not fully understand them yet, but we're seeing the effects: the weather is becoming dramatically worse.

But the world will eventually allow itself to come back into balance. The geologic record has shown it to have survived and done so after any number of previous cycles of excess and danger. And once that happens, the Pacific Ocean will be seen uniquely for what many climatologists are coming to believe it to be: a gigantic safety valve, essential to the future of the planet.

This is not to say that humankind should continue in its uncaring, greedy, polluting ways as it has done since the beginning of the Industrial Revolution two centuries ago. The amount of greenhouse gases we emit—the gas emissions from smokestacks and tail pipes that cause at least part of today's global warming problem—needs to be cut back, and drastically. That is just plain common sense: no living creature fouls its own nest in the way we have been doing for so long.

But if we do begin to act sensibly now, if we cut down on carbon-based fuels and make fewer demands on our all-too-fragile planet, maybe our world will manage to heal itself . . . this time. And thanks in large part to the unseen and unsung work of the greatest body of water we know: the Pacific.

The Pacific Ocean as the world's pacifier. Quite a notion. Maybe it truly is a pacific ocean. Maybe Ferdinand Magellan, the explorer who first named it thus, five centuries ago, was right after all.

AFTERWORD

As this book has shown, it is the pattern of alterations in the behavior of our atmosphere that produces the tangible and visible meteorological events that occur down on our planet's surface. The scale and temper of these changes has long determined the terminology we use to describe, in the broadest terms, the surface phenomena.

At the upper end of the scale there is the *climate*, which generally alters only rather slowly—though the fact that it is currently doing so at an unusually rapid pace has got everyone's attention and all brows furrowed. *Climate change*, together with its subset, *global warming*, is thought to underpin the frequency and ferocity of many of the specific events— the hurricanes, the typhoons—that this book describes.

Moving down the scale, and changing at a rather faster and more predictable rate, there are the *seasons*, which offer up annual, cyclical patterns of variations. A piece of eighteenth-century doggerel by a minor English poet named George Ellis nailed it perfectly with its twelve-word summary of the months: *Snowy, Flowy, Blowy, / Showery, Flowery, Bowery, / Hoppy, Croppy, Droppy, / Breezy, Sneezy, Freezy.* Not the same around the world, of course: it doesn't snow in January in Australia, for example, nor do the crops ripen in July in Patagonia. But for Europe and the American East, Mr. Ellis had it right enough.

Last of the trio, languishing at the lower end of the name-scale, is what we call the *weather*, with all of its quick-fire changes which so affect all of our lives, on levels that are both trivial (Do I carry an umbrella? Should I wear a scarf?) and profound (Do those clouds mean the drought will end, at last?). The weather is what affects us most immediately: Its word origins go back to the early eighth century, along with other ancient lexical creations like *bread* and *earth* and *half*. Weather is a very old word simply because, just like bread, it has for so long been an absolute essential in our lives; always has been, and always will be.

Nowadays we all like to know—or rather, believe we *need* to know—what the weather is going to do. Hence our obsession, and most particularly television's obsession, with weather prediction. An entire TV channel is devoted to anticipating it. A significant part of each radio and TV news bulletin is devoted to telling viewers what it is going to do later today or tonight and tomorrow.

While weather-watching is something people have long practiced, prediction is a newer phenomenon. The first weather forecasts were published in newspapers only in the 1860s; back then they were really no more scientific than having someone go up onto the roof, wet his finger, and hold it up into the wind. Nowadays forecasting is a business of great precision. In the United States, two brand-new computers named Luna and Surge, located in Virginia and Florida, calculate immense volumes of observed data from the atmosphere each day, and do so at unimaginable speeds. The goal is to offer predictions of the arrival of a storm, or a sudden change in the wind, to accuracies of a few minutes, or better. Commerce, public safety, school openings, vacation planning—all can rely on the data and predictions generated by this ever-improving technology.

Except—as Superstorm Sandy reminded us—Nature often has other, undisclosed plans. So while we're checking in on the data from supercomputers or watching those animated weather people and their colorful maps on our TV screens, it's also good to remember that in matters related to weather, despite all our best efforts, Nature has always had, and will always have, the upper hand.

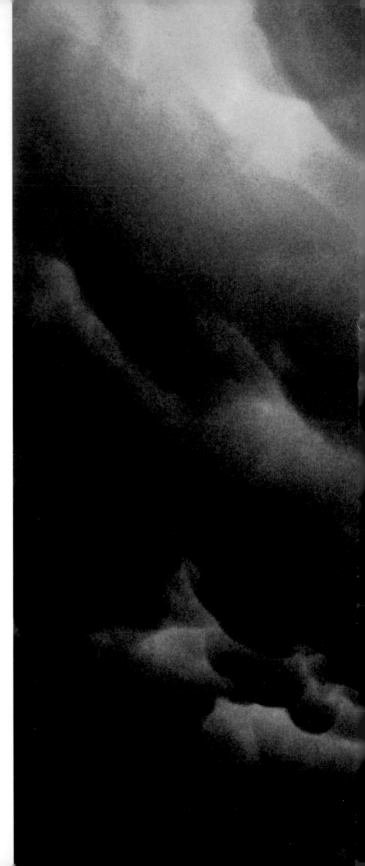

Storm clouds.

RECOMMENDED READING

For anyone wanting to delve deeper into the fascinating world of wild weather I recommend *Divine Wind: The History and Science of Hurricanes* by Kerry Emanuel (Oxford University Press, 2005). It is scientifically rigorous, easy to follow, and beautifully designed, and ranks as one of the best natural science books ever written.

I also liked the more recently published *And Soon I Heard a Roaring Wind: A Natural History of Moving Air* by Bill Streever (Little, Brown, 2016). Among other matters, Streever discusses the early history of forecasting.

For a gripping account of a great storm, read *Warning: The Story of Cyclone Tracy* by Sophie Cunningham (Melbourne: Text Publishing, 2014).

Other good books to consider:

A.D.: New Orleans After the Deluge by Josh Neufeld (Pantheon Graphic Novels, 2010)

Drowned City: Hurricane Katrina and New Orleans by Don Brown (Houghton Mifflin Harcourt Books for Young Readers, 2015)

Extreme Weather: Surviving Tornadoes, Sandstorms, Hailstorms, Blizzards, Hurricanes, and More! by Thomas M. Kostigen (National Geographic Kids, 2014)

The Power of the Sea: Tsunamis, Storm Surges, Rogue Waves, and Our Quest to Predict Disasters by Bruce Parker (Palgrave Macmillan, 2010)

Superstorm: Nine Days Inside Hurricane Sandy by Kathryn Miles (Dutton, 2014)

And don't forget two great works of fiction: *In Hazard* by Richard Hughes (New York Review of Books, 2008) and *Typhoon and Other Stories* by Joseph Conrad (Everyman's Library, 1991).

ACKNOWLEDGMENTS

Much of the research for this book was undertaken while I was living and working in Hawaii, preparing a book on the Pacific Ocean, which happens to be where most of the world's weather is generally thought to originate. I was greatly helped in the meteorological aspects of the ocean story by the staff at the Hawaii offices of the National Oceanic and Atmospheric Administration (NOAA), as well as by the staff at the US Navy's Joint Typhoon Warning Center at Pearl Harbor.

I also spent some time on the remote mid-Pacific atoll of Kwajalein, in the Marshall Islands; Mark Bradford, senior meteorologist on the atoll, proved to be a fund of fascinating information on tropical cyclones; and I wish also to thank Kevin Hamilton, an atmospheric scientist and former director of the International Pacific Research Center at the University of Hawaii. My gratitude to both is boundless.

In Tokyo I spent time at JAMSTEC, the Japanese government's principal meteorological research agency, speaking with scientists who could not have been more helpful. For arranging visits to see some of their teams of remarkable weather experts I must especially thank Ms. Mizue Iijima, who very nearly missed the plane that would take her and her husband on a well-deserved holiday in order to ensure I was given all necessary information before my visit. The JAMSTEC scientists whose work I then found especially relevant to this book were Kentaro Ando, Satomi Tomishima, and Takeshi Doi, the latter an expert on the workings of the Earth Simulator 2, the home-grown NEC supercomputer that endeavors to solve some of the more complex of the Pacific's weather puzzles.

Back in New York I must once again pay my thanks and respect to Sheila Keenan, my eagle-eyed and sharp-penciled editor at Viking Children's Books, who saw the manuscript through to completion in timely fashion, her editorial strictness invariably tempered by her ineffable Irish charm. It is a pleasure to work with her, as it is with Ken Wright, the publisher of Viking Children's Books. Specialists from the Smithsonian Institution, with whom Penguin is copublishing the books in this series, were hugely helpful in preventing me from committing any egregious errors of fact.

And I also wish to pay credit to Jim Hoover, who designed both this book and its predecessor, *When the Earth Shakes*. The look and feel of both of these volumes is a source of the greatest pride for me, and I will always be grateful that Sheila and Jim helped make them so.

INDEX

Note: Page numbers in *italics* refer to illustrations.

Lilly's Big Day

KEVIN HENKES

Greenwillow Books

An Imprint of HarperCollinsPublishers

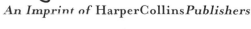

For Clara

Watercolor paints and a black pen
were used to prepare the full-color art.
The text type is 16-point Mrs. Eaves Bold.

Library of Congress Cataloging-in-Publication Data
Lilly's big day / Kevin Henkes.
"Greenwillow Books."
 p. cm.
Summary: When her teacher announces that he is getting
married, Lilly the mouse sets her heart on being the flower
girl at his wedding.
ISBN-10: 0-06-074236-4 (trade bdg.) ISBN-13: 978-0-06-074236-2 (trade bdg.)
ISBN-10: 0-06-074237-2 (lib. bdg.) ISBN-13: 978-0-06-074237-9 (lib. bdg.)
[1. Mice—Fiction. 2. Weddings—Fiction.
3. Teachers—Fiction.] I. Title.
PZ7.H389Lg 2005 [E]—dc22 2004052263

First Edition 10 9 8 7 6 5 4 3 2

One day Lilly's teacher, Mr. Slinger, announced to the class
that he was going to marry Ms. Shotwell, the school nurse.
Lilly's heart leaped. She had always wanted to be a flower girl.
"It will be the biggest day of my life," said Mr. Slinger.
"Mine, too," whispered Lilly.

At home in her room, Lilly practiced being a flower girl.

First she changed into something more appropriate.

Then she held her head high

and smiled brightly

and raised her eyebrows

and turned her head from side to side

and carried her hands proudly in front of her

and hummed "Here Comes the Bride"

and walked the length of her room very, very slowly.

Back and forth, back and forth, back and forth.

"It will be the biggest day of my life," said Lilly.

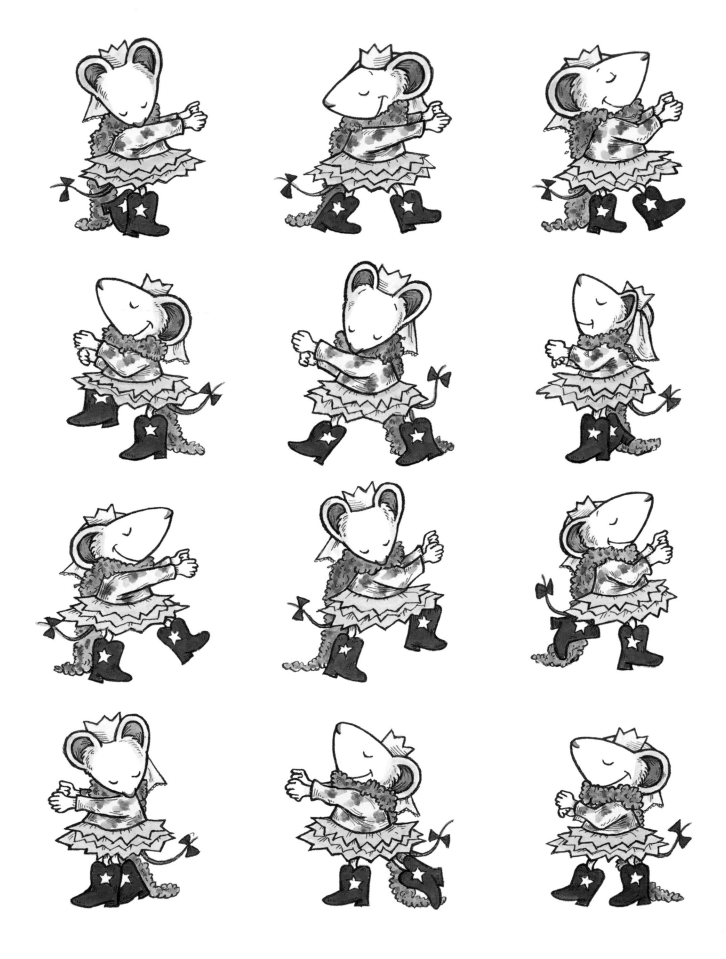

"Who are you pretending to be tonight?"
asked Lilly's mother at dinner.
"I'm not pretending," said Lilly. "I'm a flower girl."
"Who's getting married?" asked her father.
"Mr. Slinger," said Lilly.
"Really?" said her mother.
"Really?" said her father.

"Really," said Lilly. "He's going to marry Ms. Shotwell.
  He told us today. And I'm going to be the flower girl."
"You are?" said her father.
"Did Mr. Slinger ask you?" said her mother.
"Not yet," said Lilly.

At bedtime Lilly's mother said, "Lilly, there are so many students in your class. Mr. Slinger couldn't possibly pick just one to be a flower girl."

Her father said, "It wouldn't be fair."

"He probably has a niece . . . ," said her mother.

"Maybe Aunt Mona will get married someday . . . ," said her father.

"Do you understand what we're trying to say?" asked her mother.

Lilly nodded.

"Are you sure?" asked her father.

Lilly nodded again.

After her parents left her room, Lilly said, "I understand that I'm going to be a flower girl."

The next day at school during Sharing Time, Lilly said, "I've always wanted to be a flower girl. Even more than a surgeon or a diva or a hairdresser."

The following afternoon when Mr. Slinger had recess duty, Lilly picked a handful of weeds at the edge of the playground. She carried the weeds proudly in front of her and walked very, very slowly past Mr. Slinger until the bell rang. Back and forth, back and forth, back and forth.

And the morning after that, Lilly went to the Lightbulb Lab in the back of the classroom. She drew a self-portrait.

Mr. Slinger called Lilly up to his desk during Quiet Reading Time. "Lilly," he said, "I can tell that you want to be a flower girl, but unfortunately my niece, Ginger, is going to be the flower girl at my wedding."

Lilly's heart sank.

"But," said Mr. Slinger, "I also want you to know that everyone in the class will be invited to the wedding. We can all dance together at the reception. It'll be fun."

Lilly's stomach hurt.

"This seems really important to you," said Mr. Slinger.

Lilly's cheeks turned pink.

"You know . . . ," said Mr. Slinger, "I was just thinking that you might like to be Ginger's assistant. You could stand with her and keep her company until she has to walk down the aisle. You could make sure her dress isn't crooked and that she holds her flowers properly."

Lilly considered this.

"You could remind her to walk slowly," said Mr. Slinger.

Lilly considered some more.

"You could wear a corsage," said Mr. Slinger.

"Oh, all right," said Lilly, "if you really need me so much."

Lilly tried to get excited about being Ginger's assistant.

"Weddings wouldn't even exist without flower girl assistants,"
she told her baby brother, Julius.

"I have a special responsibility," she told her parents.

When her Grammy took her shopping for a new dress for the wedding, Lilly told the clerk, "A flower girl assistant is *very* important. Important *and* glamorous."

But when it really sank in that she would not be walking
down the aisle carrying a bouquet with everyone watching,
Lilly pretended that her teddy bear was Mr. Slinger.
She made him sit in the Uncooperative Chair.
"You can just stay there forever," she said.

As the wedding drew near, Mr. Slinger counted down the days
on the chalkboard.

"One day closer to the biggest day of my life," he would say.

"One day closer to the biggest day of *Ginger's* life," Lilly
would whisper.

And still, at home in her room, Lilly practiced.
  She held her head high
  and smiled brightly
  and raised her eyebrows
  and turned her head from side to side
  and carried her hands proudly in front of her
  and hummed "Here Comes the Bride"
  and walked the length of her room very, very slowly.
  Back and forth, back and forth, back and forth.

The day of the wedding finally arrived.
Lilly hoped and hoped that Ginger would have pinkeye
or a bad fever and not show up.
But she was there. And she was all ready. Her dress was
straight and she held her flowers properly.

"Are you sure you want to do this?" said Lilly.

"Yes," said Ginger.

"Are you sure you're sure?"

"Yes."

"Are you *really* sure you're sure?"

Lilly hoped and hoped that Ginger would change her mind.

But she didn't.

It was time for the ceremony to begin.

The music swelled.

Everyone stood.

The moment came for Ginger to walk down the aisle.

Ginger didn't move.

Mr. Slinger motioned her forward.

"Go," said Lilly.

Ginger was frozen.

"Now," said Lilly.

Ginger was as still as a stone.

"You can do it," said Lilly.

But Ginger couldn't.

Everyone waited. And waited. And waited.

No one knew what to do—except Lilly.

Lilly scooped up Ginger and said, "Here we go."

Then Lilly walked very, very slowly down the aisle.

She held her head high

and smiled brightly

and raised her eyebrows

and turned her head from side to side

and carried Ginger proudly in front of her.

When she reached Mr. Slinger, everyone clapped.
"I knew this would be the biggest day of my life!" said Lilly.

Lilly was so excited she barely noticed the rest of the ceremony.

The reception was great fun.

After the cake was served, Lilly coached Ginger for the next time she would be a flower girl.

"I won't be with you at every wedding," said Lilly. "I won't be able to save you every time."

Together they walked back and forth,
back and forth,
back and forth,
very, very slowly.

Soon they were dancing.

And soon after that, they were joined by Chester, Wilson,
Victor, Julius, Mr. Slinger, Ms. Shotwell, and many others.
"It's Interpretive Dance!" said Mr. Slinger.
"We're doing the Flower Girl!" said Lilly.

Lilly's family stayed at the reception until Lilly was perfectly
exhausted.

"But there's something I have to do before we go," said Lilly.

She needed to find Ginger one last time.

And when she did, she said, "Ginger, when I get married,
you can be my flower girl."